Avizandum Statutes on

Scots Criminal Law and Evidence

AVIZANDUM STATUTES

Avizandum Statutes are designed specifically to provide undergraduates at Scottish universities with legislation and, where appropriate, other core materials in a readily accessible format. All materials have been selected on the basis of their relevance to university courses and appear in updated form. The lack of annotation and commentary means that the volumes are ideal for use in examinations.

Volumes in the series:

Jonathan Hardman and Claudia Paduano (eds), *Avizandum Statutes on Scots Commercial and Consumer Law 2026–2027, 24th edition* (2026)

Jane Mair (ed), *Avizandum Statutes on Scots Family Law 2026–2027, 24th edition* (2026)

Andrew J M Steven and Scott Wortley (eds), *Avizandum Statutes on Scots Property, Trusts and Succession Law 2026–2027, 23rd edition* (2026)

Navraj Singh Ghaleigh (ed), *Avizandum Statutes on Scots Public Law, 6th edition* (2026)

Rachel McPherson (ed), *Avizandum Statutes on Scots Criminal Law and Evidence* (2026)

Laura J Macgregor and Lorna Richardson (eds), *Avizandum Legislation on the Scots Law of Obligations, 10th edition* (2025)

Elizabeth B Crawford and Janeen M Carruthers (eds), *Avizandum Legislation on International Private Law, 5th edition* (2020)

https://edinburghuniversitypress.com/series-avizandum-statutes

Avizandum Statutes on

Scots Criminal Law and Evidence

Editor

Rachel McPherson LLB (Hons), MRes (Law), PhD

Professor of Criminal Law and Evidence University of Glasgow

EDINBURGH
University Press

Edinburgh University Press is one of the leading university presses in the UK. We publish academic books and journals in our selected subject areas across the humanities and social sciences, combining cutting-edge scholarship with high editorial and production values to produce academic works of lasting importance. For more information visit our website: edinburghuniversitypress.com

Edinburgh University Press Ltd
13 Infirmary Street, Edinburgh EH1 1LT

Typeset in 12.5/15 pt, Palatino
by Deanta Global Publishing Services, Chennai, India
Printed and bound in Great Britain by Clays Ltd, Elcograf S.p.A.

A CIP record for this book is available from the British Library

ISBN 978 1 3995 7237 8 (paperback)
ISBN 978 1 3995 7236 1 (webready PDF)
ISBN 978 1 3995 7235 4 (epub)

FSC www.fsc.org MIX Paper | Supporting responsible forestry FSC® C018072

This book is printed using paper from well-managed forests, recycling and other controlled sources

EDITOR'S PREFACE

This volume is intended for undergrade students studying criminal law and the law of evidence, in either separate or combined courses. The content reflects teaching at Scottish universities and has been informed by previous guides put together by staff at the University of Glasgow, and feedback from anonymous reviewers based at other law schools in Scotland. I am grateful to these colleagues, known and unknown, for their input.

The Sexual Offences (Scotland) Act 2009 represented a significant codification of criminal law in Scotland. Since then, there has been an increase in legislation relevant to criminal law, particularly in the context of law reform aimed at addressing violence against women. The Domestic Abuse (Scotland) Act 2018 is the most notable of these and represents much of the work undertaken at summary level in Scottish courts.

I have sought to include relevant materials up to April 2026. Material not included in the statute as originally enacted has been identified by the use of square brackets.

Rachel McPherson
April 2026

CONTENTS

PART I

STATUTES

MISUSE OF DRUGS ACT 1971
(1971, c 38)

Restrictions relating to controlled drugs etc.

3 Restriction of importation and exportation of controlled drugs.

(1) Subject to subsection (2) below—

(a) the importation of a controlled drug; and

(b) the exportation of a controlled drug,

are hereby prohibited.

(2) Subsection (1) above does not apply—

(a) to the importation or exportation of a controlled drug which is for the time being excepted from paragraph (a) or, as the case may be, paragraph (b) of subsection (1) above by regulations under section 7 of this Act [or by provision made in a temporary class drug order by virtue of section 7A] ; or

(b) to the importation or exportation of a controlled drug under and in accordance with the terms of a licence issued by the Secretary of State and in compliance with any conditions attached thereto.

4 Restriction of production and supply of controlled drugs.

(1) Subject to any regulations under section 7 of this Act [, or any provision made in a temporary class drug order by virtue of section 7A,] for the time being in force, it shall not be lawful for a person—

(a) to produce a controlled drug; or

(b) to supply or offer to supply a controlled drug to another.

(2) Subject to section 28 of this Act, it is an offence for a person—

(a) to produce a controlled drug in contravention of subsection (1) above; or

(b) to be concerned in the production of such a drug in contravention of that subsection by another.

(3) Subject to section 28 of this Act, it is an offence for a person—

(a) to supply or offer to supply a controlled drug to another in contravention of subsection (1) above; or

(b) to be concerned in the supplying of such a drug to another in contravention of that subsection; or

(c) to be concerned in the making to another in contravention of that subsection of an offer to supply such a drug.

[4A Aggravation of offence of supply of controlled drug

[(1) [Subsections (2) to (8) apply] if—

(a) a court [in Scotland or Northern Ireland] is considering the seriousness of an offence under section 4(3) of this Act, and

(b) at the time the offence was committed the offender had attained the age of 18.

(2) If either of the following conditions is met the court—

(a) must treat the fact that the condition is met as an aggravating factor (that is to say, a factor that increases the seriousness of the offence), and

(b) must state in open court that the offence is so aggravated.

(3) The first condition is that the offence was committed on or in the vicinity of school premises at a relevant time.

(4) The second condition is that in connection with the commission of the offence the offender used a courier who, at the time the offence was committed, was under the age of 18.

(5) In subsection (3), a relevant time is—

(a) any time when the school premises are in use by persons under the age of 18;

(b) one hour before the start and one hour after the end of any such time.

(6) For the purposes of subsection (4), a person uses a courier in connection with an offence under section 4(3) of this Act if he causes or permits another person (the courier)—

(a) to deliver a controlled drug to a third person, or

(b) to deliver a drug related consideration to himself or a third person.

(7) For the purposes of subsection (6), a drug related consideration is a consideration of any description which—

(a) is obtained in connection with the supply of a controlled drug, or

(b) is intended to be used in connection with obtaining a controlled drug.]

(8) In this section—

'school premises' means land used for the purposes of a school excluding any land occupied solely as a dwelling by a person employed at the school; and

'school' has the same meaning—

(a) in England and Wales, as in section 4 of the Education Act 1996;

(b) in Scotland, as in section 135(1) of the Education (Scotland) Act 1980;

(c) in Northern Ireland, as in Article 2(2) of the Education and Libraries (Northern Ireland) Order 1986.

[(9) For the requirement for a court in England and Wales considering the seriousness of an offence under section 4(3) of this Act to treat certain matters as aggravating factors, see section 71 of the Sentencing Code.]]

5 Restriction of possession of controlled drugs.

(1) Subject to any regulations under section 7 of this Act for the time being in force, it shall not be lawful for a person to have a controlled drug in his possession.

(2) Subject to section 28 of this Act and to subsection (4) below, it is an offence for a person to have a controlled drug in his possession in contravention of subsection (1) above.

[(2A) Subsections (1) and (2) do not apply in relation to a temporary class drug.]

(3) Subject to section 28 of this Act, it is an offence for a person to have a controlled drug in his possession, whether lawfully or not, with intent to supply it to another in contravention of section 4(1) of this Act.

(4) In any proceedings for an offence under subsection (2) above in which it is proved that the accused had a controlled drug in his possession, it shall be a defence for him to prove—

(a) that, knowing or suspecting it to be a controlled drug, he took possession of it for the purpose of preventing another from committing or continuing to commit an offence in connection with that drug and that as soon as possible after taking possession of it he took all such steps as were reasonably open to him to destroy the drug or to deliver it into the custody of a person lawfully entitled to take custody of it; or

(b) that, knowing or suspecting it to be a controlled drug, he took possession of it for the purpose of delivering it into the custody of a person lawfully entitled to take custody of it and that as soon as possible after taking possession of it he took all such steps as were reasonably open to him to deliver it into the custody of such a person.

[(5) Subsection (4) above shall apply in the case of proceedings for an offence under section 19(1) of this Act consisting of an attempt to commit an offence under subsection (2) above as it applies in the case of proceedings for an offence under subsection (2), subject to the following modifications, that is to say—

(a) for the references to the accused having in his possession, and to his taking possession of, a controlled drug there shall be substituted respectively references to his attempting to get, and to his attempting to take, possession of such a drug; and

(b) in paragraphs (a) and (b) the words from 'and that as soon as possible' onwards shall be omitted.]

(6) Nothing in subsection (4) [or (5)] above shall prejudice any defence which it is open to a person charged with an offence under this section to raise apart from that subsection.

6 Restriction of cultivation of cannabis plant.

(1) Subject to any regulations under section 7 of this Act for the time being in force, it shall not be lawful for a person to cultivate any plant of the genus *Cannabis*.

(2) Subject to section 28 of this Act, it is an offence to cultivate any such plant in contravention subsection (1) above.

Miscellaneous and supplementary provisions

28 Proof of lack of knowledge etc. to be a defence in proceedings for certain offences.

(1) This section applies to offences under any of the following provisions of this Act, that is to say section 4(2) and (3), section 5(2) and (3), section 6(2) and section 9.

(2) Subject to subsection (3) below, in any proceedings for an offence to which this section applies it shall be a defence for the accused to prove that he neither knew of nor suspected nor had reason to suspect the existence of some fact alleged by the prosecution which it is necessary for the prosecution to prove if he is to be convicted of the offence charged.

(3) Where in any proceedings for an offence to which this section applies it is necessary, if the accused is to be convicted of the offence charged, for the prosecution to prove that some substance or product involved in the alleged offence was the controlled drug which the prosecution alleges it to have been, and it is proved that the substance or product in question was that controlled drug, the accused—

(a) shall not be acquitted of the offence charged by reason only of proving that he neither knew nor suspected nor had reason to suspect that the substance or product in question was the particular controlled drug alleged; but

(b) shall be acquitted thereof—

(i) if he proves that he neither believed nor suspected nor had reason to suspect that the substance or product in question was a controlled drug; or

(ii) if he proves that he believed the substance or product in question to be a controlled drug, or a controlled drug of a description, such that, if it had in fact been that controlled drug or a controlled drug of that description, he would not at the material time have been committing any offence to which this section applies.

(4) Nothing in this section shall prejudice any defence which it is open to a person charged with an offence to which this section applies to raise apart from this section

37 Interpretation.

(1) In this Act, except in so far as the context otherwise requires, the following expressions have the meanings hereby assigned to them respectively, that is to say:—

'the Advisory Council' means the Advisory Council on the Misuse of Drugs established under this Act;

['cannabis' (except in the expression 'cannabis resin') means any plant of the genus *Cannabis* or any part of any such plant (by whatever name designated) except that it does not include cannabis resin or any of the following products after separation from the rest of the plant, namely—

(a) mature stalk of any such plant,

(b) fibre produced from mature stalk of any such plant, and

(c) seed of any such plant;]

'cannabis resin' means the separated resin, whether crude or purified, obtained from any plant of the genus *Cannabis;*

'contravention' includes failure to comply, and 'contravene' has a corresponding meaning;

'controlled drug' has the meaning assigned by section 2 of this Act;

'corresponding law' has the meaning assigned by section 36(1) of this Act;

'dentist' means a person registered in the dentists register under the [Dentists Act 1984 […];]

['doctor' means a registered medical practitioner within the meaning of Schedule 1 to the Interpretation Act 1978;]

'enactment' includes an enactment of the Parliament of Northern Ireland;

'person lawfully conducting a retail pharmacy business' [...] means a person lawfully conducting such a business in accordance with section 69 of the Medicines Act 1968;

'pharmacist' has the same meaning as in the Medicines Act 1968;

'practitioner' (except in the expression 'veterinary practitioner') means a doctor, dentist, veterinary practitioner or veterinary surgeon;

'prepared opium' means opium prepared for smoking and includes dross and any other residues remaining after opium has been smoked;

'prescribed' means prescribed by regulations made by the Secretary of State under this Act;

'produce', where the reference is to producing a controlled drug, means producing it by manufacture, cultivation or any other method, and 'production' has a corresponding meaning;

'supplying' including distributing;

['temporary class drug order' means an order made under section 2A(1);]

'veterinary practitioner' means a person registered in the supplementary veterinary register kept under section 8 of the Veterinary Surgeons Act 1966;

'veterinary surgeon' means a person registered in the register of veterinary surgeons kept under section 2 of the Veterinary Surgeons Act 1966.

(2) References in this Act to misusing a drug are references to misusing it by taking it; and the reference in the foregoing provision to the taking of a drug is a reference to the taking of it by a human being by way of any form of self-administration, whether or not involving assistance by another.

(3) For the purposes of this Act the things which a person has in his possession shall be taken to include any thing subject to his control which is in the custody of another.

(4) Except in so far as the context otherwise requires, any reference in this Act to an enactment shall be construed as a reference to that enactment as amended or extended by or under any other enactment.

(5) […]

[…]

CONTEMPT OF COURT ACT 1981
(1981, c 49)

Strict liability

1 The strict liability rule.

In this Act 'the strict liability rule' means the rule of law whereby conduct may be treated as a contempt of court as tending to interfere with the course of justice in particular legal proceedings regardless of intent to do so.

2 Limitation of scope of strict liability.

(1) The strict liability rule applies only in relation to publications, and for this purpose 'publication' includes any speech, writing, [programme included in a cable programme service] or other communication in whatever form, which is addressed to the public at large or any section of the public.

(2) The strict liability rule applies only to a publication which creates a substantial risk that the course of justice in the proceedings in question will be seriously impeded or prejudiced.

(3) The strict liability rule applies to a publication only if the proceedings in question are active within the meaning of this section at the time of the publication.

(4) Schedule 1 applies for determining the times at which proceedings are to be treated as active within the meaning of this section.

[(5) In this section 'programme service' has the same meaning as in the Broadcasting Act 1990.]

3 Defence of innocent publication or distribution.

(1) A person is not guilty of contempt of court under the strict liability rule as the publisher of any matter to which that rule applies if at the time of publication (having taken all reasonable care) he does not know and has no reason to suspect that relevant proceedings are active.

(2) A person is not guilty of contempt of court under the strict liability rule as the distributor of a publication containing any such matter if at the time of distribution (having

taken all reasonable care) he does not know that it contains such matter and has no reason to suspect that it is likely to do so.

(3) The burden of proof of any fact tending to establish a defence afforded by this section to any person lies upon that person.

(4) […]

4 Contemporary reports of proceedings.

(1) Subject to this section a person is not guilty of contempt of court under the strict liability rule in respect of a fair and accurate report of legal proceedings held in public, published contemporaneously and in good faith.

(2) In any such proceedings the court may, where it appears to be necessary for avoiding a substantial risk of prejudice to the administration of justice in those proceedings, or in any other proceedings pending or imminent, order that the publication of any report of the proceedings, or any part of the proceedings, be postponed for such period as the court thinks necessary for that purpose.

[(2A) Where in proceedings for any offence which is an administration of justice offence for the purposes of section 54 of the Criminal Procedure and Investigations Act 1996 (acquittal tainted by an administration of justice offence) it appears to the court that there is a possibility that (by virtue of that section) proceedings may be taken against a person for an offence of which he has been acquitted, subsection (2) of this section shall apply as if those proceedings were pending or imminent.]

(3) For the purposes of subsection (1) of this section […] a report of proceedings shall be treated as published contemporaneously—

(a) in the case of a report of which publication is postponed pursuant to an order under subsection (2) of this section, if published as soon as practicable after that order expires;

[(b) in the case of a report of allocation or sending proceedings of which publication is permitted by virtue only of subsection (6) of section 52A of the Crime and Disorder Act 1998 (' the 1998 Act '), if published as soon as practicable after publication is so permitted;

(c) in the case of a report of an application of which publication is permitted by virtue only of sub-paragraph (5) or (7) of paragraph 3 of Schedule 3 to the 1998 Act, if published as soon as practicable after publication is so permitted.]

(4) [...]

5 Discussion of public affairs.

A publication made as or as part of a discussion in good faith of public affairs or other matters of general public interest is not to be treated as a contempt of court under the strict liability rule if the risk of impediment or prejudice to particular legal proceedings is merely incidental to the discussion.

Other aspects of law and procedure

8 Confidentiality of jury's deliberations [Scotland and Northern Ireland].

[(1) [In Scotland and Northern Ireland,] Subject to [subsections (1A) and (2)] below, it is a contempt of court to obtain, disclose or solicit any particulars of statements made, opinions expressed, arguments advanced or votes cast by members of a jury in the course of their deliberations in any legal proceedings.

[(1A) This section does not apply to the disclosure of any particulars made in accordance with leave granted under section 8A(1) or to the publication of any particulars so disclosed.]

(2) This section does not apply to any disclosure of any particulars—

(a) in the proceedings in question for the purpose of enabling the jury to arrive at their verdict, or in connection with the delivery of that verdict, or

(b) in evidence in any subsequent proceedings for an offence alleged to have been committed in relation to the jury in the first mentioned proceedings,

or to the publication of any particulars so disclosed.

(3) Proceedings for a contempt of court under this section (other than Scottish proceedings) shall not be instituted except by or with the consent of the Attorney General or on the motion of a court having jurisdiction to deal with it.]

[8A Research into juries

(1) The Lord Justice General may, for the purposes of research into juries in solemn proceedings, grant leave to a person to obtain, disclose, solicit or publish particulars of—

(a) statements made,

(b) opinions expressed,

(c) arguments advanced, or

(d) votes cast,

by members of a jury in the course of their deliberations in such proceedings.

(2) Leave under subsection (1) may be—

(a) granted subject to conditions,

(b) withdrawn or amended either generally or in relation to any particular matter.]

9 Use of tape recorders.

(1) Subject to subsection (4) below, it is a contempt of court—

(a) to use in court, or bring into court for use, any tape recorder or other instrument for recording sound, except with the leave of the court;

(b) to publish a recording of legal proceedings made by means of any such instrument, or any recording derived directly or indirectly from it, by playing it in the hearing of the public or any section of the public, or to dispose of it or any recording so derived, with a view to such publication;

(c) to use any such recording in contravention of any conditions of leave granted under paragraph (a).

[(d) to publish or dispose of any recording in contravention of any conditions of leave granted under subsection (1A).]

[(1A) In the case of a recording of Supreme Court proceedings, subsection (1)(b) does not apply to its publication or disposal with the leave of the Court.]

(2) Leave under paragraph (a) of subsection (1) [, or under subsection (1A),] may be granted or refused at the discretion of the court, and [if granted—

(a) may, in the case of leave under subsection (1)(a),]

be granted subject to such conditions as the court thinks proper with respect to the use of any recording made pursuant to the leave and;

[(b) may, in the case of leave under subsection (1A), be granted subject to such conditions as the Supreme Court thinks proper with respect to publication or disposal of any recording to which the leave relates; and]

where leave has been granted the court may at the like discretion withdraw or amend it either generally or in relation to any particular part of the proceedings.

(3) Without prejudice to any other power to deal with an act of contempt under paragraph (a) of subsection (1), the court may order the instrument, or any recording made with it, or both, to be forfeited; and any object so forfeited shall (unless the court otherwise determines on application by a person appearing to be the owner) be sold or otherwise disposed of in such manner as the court may direct.

(4) This section does not apply to the making or use of sound recordings for purposes of official transcripts of proceedings.

[(4A) This section does not apply to anything done in accordance with a direction under section 85A of the Courts Act 2003 (remote observation and recording of court and tribunal proceedings).]

[(5) See section 32 of the Crime and Courts Act 2013 for power to provide for further exceptions.]

10 Sources of information.

No court may require a person to disclose, nor is any person guilty of contempt of court for refusing to disclose, the source of information contained in a publication for which he is responsible, unless it be established to the satisfaction of the court that disclosure is necessary in the interests of justice or national security or for the prevention of disorder or crime.

CIVIC GOVERNMENT (SCOTLAND) ACT 1982 (1982, c 45)

PART IV
OFFENCES, POWERS OF CONSTABLES, ETC.

Offences of annoying, offensive, obstructive or dangerous behaviour

46 Soliciting and importuning by prostitutes.

(1) A prostitute (whether male or female) who for the purposes of prostitution—

(a) loiters in a public place;

(b) solicits in a public place or in any other place so as to be seen from a public place; or

(c) importunes any person who is in a public place,

shall be guilty of an offence and liable, on summary conviction, to a fine not exceeding [level 2 on the standard scale].

(2) In subsection (1) above, 'public place' has the same meaning as in section 133 of this Act but includes—

(a) any place to which at the material time the public are permitted to have access, whether on payment or otherwise; and

(b) any public conveyance other than a taxi or hire car within the meaning of section 23 of this Act.

47 Urinating etc.

Any person who urinates or defecates in such circumstances as to cause, or to be likely to cause, annoyance to any other person shall be guilty of an offence and liable, on summary conviction, to a fine not exceeding [level 2 on the standard scale].

49 Dangerous and annoying creatures.

(1) Any person who suffers or permits any creature in his charge to cause danger or injury to any other person who is in a public place or to give such person reasonable cause for alarm or annoyance shall be guilty of an offence and liable,

on summary conviction, to a fine not exceeding [level 2 on the standard scale].

(2) A district court may, if satisfied that any creature kept in the vicinity of any place where a person resides is giving that person, while in that place, reasonable cause for annoyance, make an order requiring the person keeping the creature to take, within such period as may be specified in the order, such steps (short of destruction of the creature) to prevent the continuance of the annoyance as may be so specified.

(3) An application to a district court for an order under subsection (2) above may be made by any person.

(4) Any person who fails to comply with an order under subsection (2) above shall be guilty of an offence and liable, on summary conviction, to a fine not exceeding [level 3 on the standard scale].

(5) The fact that there is a licence under the Dangerous Wild Animals Act 1976 in respect of a creature shall not of itself afford a defence in proceedings under this section relating to that creature.

(6) Where a court convicts a person of an offence under this section or discharges him absolutely [...], it may, whether or not (in the case of conviction) it imposes a penalty under subsection (1) or (4) above—

(a) subject to subsection (8) below, make such order as it sees fit as to the disposal of the creature to which the proceedings relate;

(b) authorise a constable, in pursuance of such an order, to take possession of the creature.

(7) An order under subsection (6) above may, subject to any enactment relating to the protection or conservation of living things, be for the destruction of the creature to which it relates.

(8) No creature disposed of under an order under subsection (6) above shall be given or sold for the purposes of vivisection.

50 Drunkenness.

(1) Any person who, while not in the care or protection of a suitable person, is, in a public place, drunk and incapable of taking care of himself shall be guilty of an offence and liable, on summary conviction, to a fine not exceeding [level 2 on the standard scale].

(2) Any person who is drunk in a public place while in charge of a child under the age of 10 shall be guilty of an offence and liable, on summary conviction, to a fine not exceeding [level 2 on the standard scale].

(3) For the purposes of subsection (2) above, if a child appears to the court to be under the age of 10, the child shall be deemed to be under that age unless the contrary is proved.

(4) A constable may arrest a person for contravening subsection (2) above if he has reasonable cause to believe that the child in the charge of that person is under the age of 10.

(5) Any person who is drunk in a public place while in possession of a firearm (including a crossbow, airgun, air rifle or air pistol) shall be guilty of an offence and liable, on summary conviction, to a fine not exceeding [level 2 on the standard scale].

(6) In this section, 'public place' has the same meaning as in section 133 of this Act but includes—

(a) any place to which at the material time the public are permitted to have access, whether on payment or otherwise; and

(b) any public conveyance other than a taxi or hire car within the meaning of section 23 of this Act.

51 Obscene material.

(1) Subject to subsection (4) below, any person who displays any obscene material in any public place or in any other place where it can be seen by the public shall be guilty of an offence under this section.

(2) Subject to subsection (4) below, any person who publishes, sells or distributes or, with a view to its eventual sale

or distribution, makes, prints, has or keeps any obscene material shall be guilty of an offence under this section.

[(2A) Subject to subsection (4) below, any person who—

(a) is responsible for the inclusion of any obscene material in a programme included in a programme service; or

(b) with a view to its eventual inclusion in a programme so included, makes, prints, has or keeps any obscene material,

shall be guilty of an offence under this section.]

[(3) A person guilty of an offence under this section is liable—

(a) on summary conviction, to imprisonment for a period not exceeding 12 months or to a fine not exceeding the statutory maximum or to both, or

(b) on conviction on indictment—

(i) in a case where the obscene material is or includes an extreme pornographic image, to imprisonment for a period not exceeding 5 years or to a fine or to both, or

(ii) in any other case, to imprisonment for a period not exceeding 3 years or to a fine or to both.]

(4) A person shall not be convicted of an offence under this section if he proves that he had used all due diligence to avoid committing the offence.

(5) Under an indictment for or on a complaint of a breach of subsection (1) above, the court may, if satisfied that the person accused is guilty of an offence under section 1(1) of the Indecent Displays (Control) Act 1981 (offence of public display of indecent matter), convict him of a breach of the said section 1(1).

(6) Nothing in this section applies in relation to any matter—

(a) [...]

(b) included in a performance of a play (within the meaning of the Theatres Act 1968).

(7) For section 5(4)(b) of the Indecent Displays (Control) Act 1981 (saving) there shall be substituted the following—

'(b) section 51 of the Civic Government (Scotland) Act 1982.'

(8) In this section—

['extreme pornographic image' is to be construed in accordance with section 51A;]

'material' includes any book, magazine, bill, paper, print, film, tape, disc or other kind of recording (whether of sound or visual images or both), photograph, drawing, painting, representation, model or figure [...];

'photograph' includes the negative as well as the positive version;

'public place' has the same meaning as in section 133 of this Act except that it includes any place to which at the material time the public are permitted to have access, whether on payment or otherwise;

[...]

['programme' and 'programme service' have the same meaning as in the Broadcasting Act 1990;]

and the reference to publishing includes a reference to [...] playing, projecting or otherwise reproducing [, or, where the material is data stored electronically, transmitting that data].

[51A Extreme pornography

(1) A person who is in possession of an extreme pornographic image is guilty of an offence under this section.

(2) An extreme pornographic image is an image which is all of the following—

(a) obscene,

(b) pornographic,

(c) extreme.

(3) An image is pornographic if it is of such a nature that it must reasonably be assumed to have been made solely or principally for the purpose of sexual arousal.

(4) Where (as found in the person's possession) an image forms part of a series of images, the question of whether the image is pornographic is to be determined by reference to—

(a) the image itself, and

(b) where the series of images is such as to be capable of providing a context for the image, its context within the series of images,

and reference may also be had to any sounds accompanying the image or the series of images.

(5) So, for example, where—

(a) an image forms an integral part of a narrative constituted by a series of images, and

(b) having regard to those images as a whole, they are not of such a nature that they must reasonably be assumed to have been made solely or principally for the purpose of sexual arousal,

the image may, by virtue of being part of that narrative, be found not to be pornographic (even if it may have been found to be pornographic where taken by itself).

(6) An image is extreme if it depicts, in an explicit and realistic way any of the following—

(a) an act which takes or threatens a person's life,

(b) an act which results, or is likely to result, in a person's severe injury,

(c) rape or other non-consensual penetrative sexual activity,

(d) sexual activity involving (directly or indirectly) a human corpse,

(e) an act which involves sexual activity between a person and an animal (or the carcase of an animal).

(7) In determining whether (as found in the person's possession) an image depicts an act mentioned in subsection (6), reference may be had to—

(a) how the image is or was described (whether the description is part of the image itself or otherwise),

(b) any sounds accompanying the image,

(c) where the image forms an integral part of a narrative constituted by a series of images—

(i) any sounds accompanying the series of images,

(ii) the context provided by that narrative.

(8) A person guilty of an offence under this section is liable—

(a) on summary conviction, to imprisonment for a period not exceeding 12 months or to a fine not exceeding the statutory maximum or to both,

(b) on conviction on indictment, to imprisonment for a period not exceeding 3 years or to a fine or to both.

(9) In this section, an 'image' is—

(a) a moving or still image (made by any means), or

(b) data (stored by any means) which is capable of conversion into such an image.

51B Extreme pornography: excluded images

(1) An offence is not committed under section 51A if the image is an excluded image.

(2) An 'excluded image' is an image which is all or part of a classified work.

(3) An image is not an excluded image where—

(a) it has been extracted from a classified work, and

(b) it must be reasonably be assumed to have been extracted (whether with or without other images) from the work solely or principally for the purpose of sexual arousal.

(4) In determining whether (as found in the person's possession) the image was extracted from the work for the purpose mentioned in subsection (3)(b), reference may be had to—

(a) how the image was stored,

(b) how the image is or was described (whether the description is part of the image itself or otherwise),

(c) any sounds accompanying the image,

(d) where the image forms an integral part of a narrative constituted by a series of images—

(i) any sounds accompanying the series of images,

(ii) the context provided by that narrative.

(5) In this section—

'classified work' means a video work in respect of which a classification certificate has been issued by a designated authority,

'classification certificate' and 'video work' have the same meanings as in the Video Recordings Act 1984 (c.39),

'designated authority' means an authority which has been designated by the Secretary of State under section 4 of that Act,

'extract' includes an extract of a single image,

'image' is to be construed in accordance with section 51A.

51C Extreme pornography: defences

(1) Where a person ('A') is charged with an offence under section 51A, it is a defence for A to prove one or more of the matters mentioned in subsection (2).

(2) The matters are—

(a) that A had a legitimate reason for being in possession of the image concerned,

(b) that A had not seen the image concerned and did not know, nor had any cause to suspect, it to be an extreme pornographic image,

(c) that A—

(i) was sent the image concerned without any prior request having been made by or on behalf of A, and

(ii) did not keep it for an unreasonable time.

(3) Where A is charged with an offence under section 51A, it is a defence for A to prove that—

(a) A directly participated in the act depicted, and

(b) subsection (4) applies.

(4) This subsection applies—

(a) in the case of an image which depicts an act described in subsection (6)(a) of that section, if the act depicted did not actually take or threaten a person's life,

(b) in the case of an image which depicts an act described in subsection (6)(b) of that section, if the act depicted did not actually result in (nor was it actually likely to result in) a person's severe injury,

(c) in the case of an image which depicts an act described in subsection (6)(c) of that section, if the act depicted did not actually involve non-consensual activity,

(d) in the case of an image which depicts an act described in subsection (6)(d) of that section, if what is depicted as a human corpse was not in fact a corpse,

(e) in the case of an image which depicts an act described in subsection (6)(e) of that section, if what is depicted as an animal (or the carcase of an animal) was not in fact an animal (or a carcase).

(5) The defence under subsection (3) is not available if A shows, gives or offers for sale the image to any person who was not also a direct participant in the act depicted.

(6) In this section 'image' and 'extreme pornographic image' are to be construed in accordance with section 51A.]

52 Indecent photographs etc. of children.

(1) Any person who—

(a) takes, or permits to be taken [or makes], any indecent photograph [or pseudo-photograph of a child]

(b) distributes or shows such an indecent photograph [or pseudo-photograph];

(c) has in his possession such an indecent photograph [or pseudo-photograph] with a view to its being distributed or shown by himself or others: or

(d) publishes or causes to be published any advertisement likely to be understood as conveying that the advertiser distributes or shows such an indecent photograph [or pseudo-photograph], or intends to do so

shall be guilty of an offence under this section.

(2) [In subsection (1) above 'child' means, subject to subsection (2B) below, a person under the age of [18]; and] in proceedings under this section a person is to be taken as having been a child at any material time if it appears from the evidence as a whole that he was then under the age of [18].

[(2A) In this section, 'pseudo-photograph' means an image, whether produced by computer-graphics or otherwise howsoever, which appears to be a photograph.

(2B) If the impression conveyed by a pseudo-photograph is that the person shown is a child, the pseudo-photograph shall be treated for all purposes of this Act as showing a child and so shall a pseudo-photograph where the predominant impression conveyed is that the person shown is a child notwithstanding that some of the physical characteristics shown are those of an adult.

(2C) In this section, references to an indecent pseudo-photograph include—

(a) a copy of an indecent pseudo-photograph;

(b) data stored on a computer disc or by other electronic means which is capable of conversion into [an indecent pseudo-photograph].]

(3) A person guilty of an offence under this section shall be liable—

(a) on summary conviction, to imprisonment for a period not exceeding [6 months] or to a fine not exceeding the prescribed sum within the meaning of [section 225(8) of the Criminal Procedure (Scotland) Act 1995] (at the passing of this Act £1,000) or to both;

(b) on conviction on indictment, to imprisonment for a period not exceeding [[10 years]] or to a fine or to both.

(4) For the purposes of this section, a person is to be regarded as distributing an indecent photograph [or pseudo-photograph] if he parts with possession of it to, or exposes or offers it for acquisition by, another person.

[(4A) Where a person is charged with an offence under subsection (1)(a) of making an indecent photograph or pseudo-photograph of a child, it shall be a defence for the person to prove that—

(a) at the time of the offence charged, the person was a member of OFCOM, employed or engaged by OFCOM, or assisting OFCOM in the exercise of any of their online safety functions (within the meaning of section 235 of the Online Safety Act 2023), and

(b) the person made the photograph or pseudo-photograph for the purposes of OFCOM's exercise of any of those functions.]

(5) Where a person is charged with an offence under subsection (1)(b) or (c) above, it shall be a defence for him to prove—

(a) that he had a legitimate reason for distributing or showing the photograph [or pseudo-photograph] or (as the case may be) having it in his possession; or

(b) that he had not himself seen the photograph [or pseudo-photograph] and did not know, nor had any cause to suspect, it to be indecent.

(6) In paragraph 2 of the Schedule to the Visiting Forces Act 1952 (offences against the person in the case of which a member of a visiting force is in certain circumstances not liable to be tried by a United Kingdom court) the word 'and' immediately preceding sub-paragraph (b)(iii) shall be omitted and after the said sub-paragraph (b)(iii) there shall be added—

'(iv) section 52(1)(a) of the Civic Government (Scotland) Act 1982.'

(7) [...]

(8) In this section—

(a) references to an indecent photograph include an indecent film, a copy of an indecent photograph or film and an indecent photograph comprised in a film;

(b) a photograph (including one comprised in a film) shall, if it shows a child and is indecent, be treated for all purposes of this section as an indecent photograph of a child;

[(c) references to a photograph include—

(i) the negative as well as the positive version; and

(ii) data stored on a computer disc or by other electronic means which is capable of conversion into a photograph.]

(d) 'film' includes any form of video-recording.

[(e) 'OFCOM' means the Office of Communications.]

[(9) In this section, references to a photograph also include a tracing or other image, whether made by electronic or other means (of whatever nature), which is not itself a photograph or pseudo-photograph but which is derived from the whole or part of a photograph or pseudo-photograph (or a combination of either or both).

(10) And subsection (2B) applies in relation to such an image as it applies in relation to a pseudo-photograph.]

[52A Possession of indecent photographs of children.

(1) It is an offence for a person to have any indecent photograph [or pseudo-photograph of a child] in his possession.

(2) Where a person is charged with an offence under subsection (1), it shall be a defence for him to prove—

(a) that he had a legitimate reason for having the photograph [or pseudo-photograph] in his possession; or

(b) that he had not himself seen the photograph [or pseudo-photograph] and did not know, nor had any cause to suspect, it to be indecent; or

(c) that the photograph [or pseudo-photograph] was sent to him without any prior request made by him or on his behalf and that he did not keep it for an unreasonable time.

(3) A person shall be liable

[(a)] on summary conviction of an offence under this section to [imprisonment for a period not exceeding 6 months or to] a fine not exceeding level 5 on the standard scale ['or to both.'].

[(b) on conviction on indictment of such an offence to imprisonment for a period not exceeding 5 years or to a fine or to both.]

(4) Subsections (2) [to (2C)] [and (8) to (10)] of section 52 of this Act shall have effect for the purposes of this section as they have for the purposes of that section.]

[52B Sections 52 and 52A: exceptions for photographs of 16 and 17 year olds

(1) If subsection (2) below applies, the accused is not guilty of an offence under section 52(1)(a) of this Act of taking or making an indecent photograph of a child.

(2) This subsection applies if—

(a) either—

(i) the photograph was of the child aged 16 or over; or

(ii) the accused reasonably believed that to be so;

(b) at the time of the offence charged or at the time when the accused obtained the photograph, the accused and the child were—

(i) married to or civil partners of each other; or

(ii) partners in an established relationship; and

(c) either—

(i) the child consented to the photograph being taken or made; or

(ii) the accused reasonably believed that to be so.

(3) If subsection (4) below applies, the accused is not guilty of an offence under section 52(1)(b) of this Act relating to an indecent photograph of a child.

(4) This subsection applies if—

(a) either—

(i) the photograph was of the child aged 16 or over; or

(ii) the accused reasonably believed that to be so;

(b) at the time of the offence charged or at the time when the accused obtained the photograph, the accused and the child were—

(i) married to or civil partners of each other; or

(ii) partners in an established relationship;

(c) either—

(i) the child consented to the photograph's being taken or made; or

(ii) the accused reasonably believed that to be so; and

(d) the showing or distributing of the photograph was only to the child.

(5) If subsection (6) below applies, the accused is not guilty of an offence under section 52(1)(c) of this Act relating to an indecent photograph of a child.

(6) This subsection applies if—

(a) either—

(i) the photograph was of the child aged 16 or over; or

(ii) the accused reasonably believed that to be so;

(b) at the time of the offence charged or at the time when the accused obtained the photograph, the accused and the child were—

(i) married to or civil partners of each other; or

(ii) partners in an established relationship;

(c) either—

(i) the child consented to the photograph's being in the accused's possession; or

(ii) the accused reasonably believed that to be so; and

(d) the accused had the photograph in his possession with a view to its being distributed or shown only to the child.

(7) If subsection (8) below applies, the accused is not guilty of an offence under section 52A of this Act relating to an indecent photograph of a child.

(8) This subsection applies if—

(a) either—

(i) the photograph was of the child aged 16 or over; or

(ii) the accused reasonably believed that to be so;

(b) at the time of the offence charged or at the time when the accused obtained the photograph, the accused and the child were—

(i) married to or civil partners of each other; or

(ii) partners in an established relationship; and

(c) either—

(i) the child consented to the photograph's being in the accused's possession; or

(ii) the accused reasonably believed that to be so.

(9) Subsections (2), (4), (6) and (8) above apply whether the photograph showed the child alone or with the accused, but not if it showed any other person.

52C Section 52B: proof of exceptions

(1) This section applies for the purpose of determining whether a matter within a paragraph of section 52B(2), (4), (6) or (8) of this Act is the case.

(2) If sufficient evidence is adduced to raise an issue as to whether the matter is the case, it shall be held to be the case, except where subsection (3) below applies.

(3) This subsection applies where the prosecution proves beyond reasonable doubt that the matter is not the case.

(4) Otherwise, the matter shall be held not to be the case.]

ROAD TRAFFIC ACT 1988
(1988, c 52)

PART I
PRINCIPAL ROAD SAFETY PROVISIONS

[1 Causing death by dangerous driving.

A person who causes the death of another person by driving a mechanically propelled vehicle dangerously on a road or other public place is guilty of an offence.]

[1A Causing serious injury by dangerous driving

(1) A person who causes serious injury to another person by driving a mechanically propelled vehicle dangerously on a road or other public place is guilty of an offence.

(2) In this section 'serious injury' means—

(a) in England and Wales, physical harm which amounts to grievous bodily harm for the purposes of the Offences against the Person Act 1861, and

(b) in Scotland, severe physical injury.]

[2 Dangerous driving.

A person who drives a mechanically propelled vehicle dangerously on a road or other public place is guilty of an offence.]

[2A Meaning of dangerous driving.

(1) For the purposes of sections 1 [, 1A] and 2 above a person is to be regarded as driving dangerously if (and, subject to subsection (2) below, only if)—

(a) the way he drives falls far below what would be expected of a competent and careful driver, and

(b) it would be obvious to a competent and careful driver that driving in that way would be dangerous.

[But this subsection does not apply where subsection (1B) applies.]

[(1A) Subsection (1B) applies where a designated person—

(a) is driving for police purposes (subject to subsections (1E) and (1F)), and

(b) has undertaken prescribed training.

(1B) For the purposes of sections 1, 1A and 2 above, the designated person is to be regarded as driving dangerously if (and, subject to subsection (2) below, only if)—

(a) the way the person drives falls far below what would be expected of a competent and careful constable who has undertaken the same prescribed training, and

(b) it would be obvious to such a competent and careful constable that driving in that way would be dangerous.

(1C) In subsections (1A) and (1B) 'designated person' means—

(a) a constable,

(b) a member of staff appointed by the chief officer of police of a police force in England and Wales,

(c) a member of staff appointed by a local policing body and employed to assist a police force in England and Wales,

(d) a member of staff appointed by the Scottish Police Authority under section 26(1) of the Police and Fire Reform (Scotland) Act 2012 (asp 8),

(e) an employee of the British Transport Police Authority appointed under section 27 of the Railways and Transport Safety Act 2003,

(f) a person employed or engaged by—

(i) a chief officer of police,

(ii) the British Transport Police Authority,

(iii) the Civil Nuclear Police Authority,

(iv) the chief constable for the Ministry of Defence Police, or

(v) the Scottish Police Authority,

to train a person within any of paragraphs (a) to (e) to drive for police purposes,

(g) a person employed or engaged by a person within paragraph (f)(i) to (v) to train another person to carry out training of the kind mentioned in that paragraph,

(h) a National Crime Agency officer, or

(i) a person engaged by the National Crime Agency—

(i) to train a National Crime Agency officer to drive for law enforcement purposes, or

(ii) to train another person to carry out training of the kind mentioned in sub-paragraph (i).

(1D) In subsection (1C)(a) 'constable' does not include a port constable within the meaning of section 7 of the Marine Navigation Act 2013 or a person appointed to act as a constable under provision made by virtue of section 16 of the Harbours Act 1964.

(1E) In the case of a National Crime Agency officer, the reference in subsection (1A)(a) to driving for police purposes is to be read as a reference to driving for law enforcement purposes.

(1F) In the case of a person within paragraph (i) of subsection (1C), the reference in subsection (1A)(a) to driving for police purposes is to be read as a reference to driving for the purpose of the training mentioned in that paragraph.]

(2) A person is also to be regarded as driving dangerously for the purposes of sections 1 [, 1A] and 2 above if it would be obvious to a competent and careful driver that driving the vehicle in its current state would be dangerous.

(3) In subsections (1) [, (1B)] and (2) above 'dangerous' refers to danger either of injury to any person or of serious damage to property; and in determining for the purposes of those subsections what would be expected of, or obvious to, a competent and careful driver [or constable (as the case may be)] in a particular case, regard shall be had not only to the circumstances of which he could be expected to be aware but also to any circumstances shown to have been within the knowledge of the accused.

(4) In determining for the purposes of subsection (2) above the state of a vehicle, regard may be had to anything attached to or carried on or in it and to the manner in which it is attached or carried.]

[2B Causing death by careless, or inconsiderate, driving

A person who causes the death of another person by driving a mechanically propelled vehicle on a road or other public place without due care and attention, or without reasonable consideration for other persons using the road or place, is guilty of an offence.]

[2C Causing serious injury by careless, or inconsiderate, driving

(1) A person who causes serious injury to another person by driving a mechanically propelled vehicle on a road or other public place without due care and attention, or without reasonable consideration for other persons using the road or place, is guilty of an offence.

(2) In this section 'serious injury' means—

(a) in England and Wales, physical harm which amounts to grievous bodily harm for the purposes of the Offences against the Person Act 1861, and

(b) in Scotland, severe physical injury.]

[3 Careless, and inconsiderate, driving.

If a person drives a mechanically propelled vehicle on a road or other public place without due care and attention, or without reasonable consideration for other persons using the road or place, he is guilty of an offence.]

[3ZA Meaning of careless, or inconsiderate, driving

(1) This section has effect for the purposes of sections 2B [, 2C] and 3 above and section 3A below.

(2) A person is to be regarded as driving without due care and attention if (and only if) the way he drives falls below what would be expected of a competent and careful driver. [But this subsection does not apply where subsection (2B) applies.]

[(2A) Subsection (2B) applies where a designated person—

(a) is driving for police purposes (subject to subsections (2E) and (2F)), and

(b) has undertaken prescribed training.

(2B) The designated person is to be regarded as driving without due care and attention if (and only if) the way the person drives falls below what would be expected of a competent and careful constable who has undertaken the same prescribed training.

(2C) In subsections (2A) and (2B) 'designated person' means—

(a) a constable,

(b) a member of staff appointed by the chief officer of police of a police force in England and Wales,

(c) a member of staff appointed by a local policing body and employed to assist a police force in England and Wales,

(d) a member of staff appointed by the Scottish Police Authority under section 26(1) of the Police and Fire Reform (Scotland) Act 2012 (asp 8),

(e) an employee of the British Transport Police Authority appointed under section 27 of the Railways and Transport Safety Act 2003,

(f) a person employed or engaged by—

(i) a chief officer of police,

(ii) the British Transport Police Authority,

(iii) the Civil Nuclear Police Authority,

(iv) the chief constable for the Ministry of Defence Police, or

(v) the Scottish Police Authority,

to train a person within any of paragraphs (a) to (e) to drive for police purposes,

(g) a person employed or engaged by a person within paragraph (f)(i) to (v) to train another person to carry out training of the kind mentioned in that paragraph,

(h) a National Crime Agency officer, or

(i) a person engaged by the National Crime Agency—

(i) to train a National Crime Agency officer to drive for law enforcement purposes, or

(ii) to train another person to carry out training of the kind mentioned in sub-paragraph (i).

(2D) In subsection (2C)(a) 'constable' does not include a port constable within the meaning of section 7 of the Marine Navigation Act 2013 or a person appointed to act as a constable under provision made by virtue of section 16 of the Harbours Act 1964.

(2E) In the case of a National Crime Agency officer, the reference in subsection (2A)(a) to driving for police purposes is to be read as a reference to driving for law enforcement purposes.

(2F) In the case of a person within paragraph (i) of subsection (2C), the reference in subsection (2A)(a) to driving for police purposes is to be read as a reference to driving for the purpose of the training mentioned in that paragraph.]

(3) In determining for the purposes of subsection (2) [or (2B)] above what would be expected of a careful and competent driver [or constable (as the case may be)] in a particular case, regard shall be had not only to the circumstances of which he could be expected to be aware but also to any circumstances shown to have been within the knowledge of the accused.

(4) A person is to be regarded as driving without reasonable consideration for other persons only if those persons are inconvenienced by his driving.]

[3ZB Causing death by driving: unlicensed [...] or uninsured drivers

A person is guilty of an offence under this section if he causes the death of another person by driving a motor vehicle on a road and, at the time when he is driving, the circumstances are such that he is committing an offence under—

(a) section 87(1) of this Act (driving otherwise than in accordance with a licence),

(b) [...] or

(c) section 143 of this Act (using motor vehicle while uninsured [...]).]

[3ZC Causing death by driving: disqualified drivers

A person is guilty of an offence under this section if he or she—

(a) causes the death of another person by driving a motor vehicle on a road, and

(b) at that time, is committing an offence under section 103(1)(b) of this Act (driving while disqualified).

3ZD Causing serious injury by driving: disqualified drivers

(1) A person is guilty of an offence under this section if he or she—

(a) causes serious injury to another person by driving a motor vehicle on a road, and

(b) at that time, is committing an offence under section 103(1)(b) of this Act (driving while disqualified).

(2) In this section 'serious injury' means—

(a) in England and Wales, physical harm which amounts to grievous bodily harm for the purposes of the Offences against the Person Act 1861, and

(b) in Scotland, severe physical injury.]

[3A Causing death by careless driving when under influence of drink or drugs.

(1) If a person causes the death of another person by driving a mechanically propelled vehicle on a road or other public place without due care and attention, or without reasonable consideration for other persons using the road or place, and—

(a) he is, at the time when he is driving, unfit to drive through drink or drugs, or

(b) he has consumed so much alcohol that the proportion of it in his breath, blood or urine at that time exceeds the prescribed limit, or

[(ba) he has in his body a specified controlled drug and the proportion of it in his blood or urine at that time exceeds the specified limit for that drug, or]

(c) he is, within 18 hours after that time, required to provide a specimen in pursuance of section 7 of this Act, but without reasonable excuse fails to provide it,[or

(d) he is required by a constable to give his permission for a laboratory test of a specimen of blood taken from him under section 7A of this Act, but without reasonable excuse fails to do so,]

he is guilty of an offence.

(2) For the purposes of this section a person shall be taken to be unfit to drive at any time when his ability to drive properly is impaired.

(3) Subsection (1)(b)[, (ba)][, (c) and (d)] above shall not apply in relation to a person driving a mechanically propelled vehicle other than a motor vehicle.]

Motor vehicles: drink and drugs

4 Driving, or being in charge, when under influence of drink or drugs.

(1) A person who, when driving or attempting to drive a [mechanically propelled vehicle] on a road or other public place, is unfit to drive through drink or drugs is guilty of an offence.

(2) Without prejudice to subsection (1) above, a person who, when in charge of a [mechanically propelled vehicle] which is on a road or other public place, is unfit to drive through drink or drugs is guilty of an offence.

(3) For the purposes of subsection (2) above, a person shall be deemed not to have been in charge of a [mechanically propelled vehicle] if he proves that at the material time the circumstances were such that there was no likelihood of his driving it so long as he remained unfit to drive through drink or drugs.

(4) The court may, in determining whether there was such a likelihood as is mentioned in subsection (3) above, disregard any injury to him and any damage to the vehicle.

(5) For the purposes of this section, a person shall be taken to be unfit to drive if his ability to drive properly is for the time being impaired.

(6) [A constable may arrest a person without warrant if he has reasonable cause to suspect that that person is or has been committing an offence under this section.]

(7) [For the purpose of arresting a person under the power conferred by subsection (6) above, a constable may enter (if need be by force) any place where that person is or where the constable, with reasonable cause, suspects him to be.]

(8) […]

5 Driving or being in charge of a motor vehicle with alcohol concentration above prescribed limit.

(1) If a person—

(a) drives or attempts to drive a motor vehicle on a road or other public place, or

(b) is in charge of a motor vehicle on a road or other public place,

after consuming so much alcohol that the proportion of it in his breath, blood or urine exceeds the prescribed limit he is guilty of an offence.

(2) It is a defence for a person charged with an offence under subsection (1)(b) above to prove that at the time he is alleged to have committed the offence the circumstances were such that there was no likelihood of his driving the vehicle whilst the proportion of alcohol in his breath, blood or urine remained likely to exceed the prescribed limit.

(3) The court may, in determining whether there was such a likelihood as is mentioned in subsection (2) above, disregard any injury to him and any damage to the vehicle.

[5A Driving or being in charge of a motor vehicle with concentration of specified controlled drug above specified limit

(1) This section applies where a person ('D')—

(a) drives or attempts to drive a motor vehicle on a road or other public place, or

(b) is in charge of a motor vehicle on a road or other public place,

and there is in D's body a specified controlled drug.

(2) D is guilty of an offence if the proportion of the drug in D's blood or urine exceeds the specified limit for that drug.

(3) It is a defence for a person ('D') charged with an offence under this section to show that—

(a) the specified controlled drug had been prescribed or supplied to D for medical or dental purposes,

(b) D took the drug in accordance with any directions given by the person by whom the drug was prescribed or supplied, and with any accompanying instructions (so far as consistent with any such directions) given by the manufacturer or distributor of the drug, and

(c) D's possession of the drug immediately before taking it was not unlawful under section 5(1) of the Misuse of Drugs Act 1971 (restriction of possession of controlled drugs) because of an exemption in regulations made under section 7 of that Act (authorisation of activities otherwise unlawful under foregoing provisions).

(4) The defence in subsection (3) is not available if D's actions were—

(a) contrary to any advice, given by the person by whom the drug was prescribed or supplied, about the amount of time that should elapse between taking the drug and driving a motor vehicle, or

(b) contrary to any accompanying instructions about that matter (so far as consistent with any such advice) given by the manufacturer or distributor of the drug.

(5) If evidence is adduced that is sufficient to raise an issue with respect to the defence in subsection (3), the court must assume that the defence is satisfied unless the prosecution proves beyond reasonable doubt that it is not.

(6) It is a defence for a person ('D') charged with an offence by virtue of subsection (1)(b) to prove that at the time D is alleged to have committed the offence the circumstances were such that there was no likelihood of D driving the vehicle

whilst the proportion of the specified controlled drug in D's blood or urine remained likely to exceed the specified limit for that drug.

(7) The court may, in determining whether there was such a likelihood, disregard any injury to D and any damage to the vehicle.

(8) In this section, and in sections 3A, 6C(1), 6D and 10, 'specified' means specified in regulations made—

(a) by the Secretary of State, in relation to driving or attempting to drive, or being in charge of a vehicle, in England and Wales;

(b) by the Scottish Ministers, in relation to driving or attempting to drive, or being in charge of a vehicle, in Scotland.

(9) A limit specified under subsection (2) may be zero.]

CRIMINAL LAW (CONSOLIDATION) (SCOTLAND) ACT 1995
(1995, c 39)

PART I
SEXUAL OFFENCES

Incest and related offences

1 Incest.

(1) Any male person who has sexual intercourse with a person related to him in a degree specified in column 1 of the Table set out at the end of this subsection, or any female person who has sexual intercourse with a person related to her in a degree specified in column 2 of that Table, shall be guilty of incest, unless the accused proves that he or she—

(a) did not know and had no reason to suspect that the person with whom he or she had sexual intercourse was related in a degree so specified; or

(b) did not consent to have sexual intercourse, or to have sexual intercourse with that person; or

(c) was married to that person, at the time when the sexual intercourse took place, by a marriage entered into outside Scotland and recognised as valid by Scots law.

Table
Degrees of Relationship

Column 1	**Column 2**
1. Relationships by consanguinity	
Mother	Father
Daughter	Son
Grandmother	Grandfather
Grand-daughter	Grandson
Sister	Brother
Aunt	Uncle
Niece	Nephew
Great grandmother	Great grandfather
Great grand-daughter	Great grandson

2. Relationships by adoption

Adoptive mother or former adoptive mother.	Adoptive father or former adoptive father.
Adopted daughter or former adopted daughter.	Adopted son or former adopted son.

[3. Relationships by virtue of Part 2 of the Human Fertilisation and Embryology Act 2008

Mother	Father
Daughter	Son
Second female parent by virtue of section 42 or 43 of that Act]	

(2) For the purpose of this section, a degree of relationship exists in the case of a degree specified in paragraph 1 of the Table—

(a) whether it is of the full blood or the half blood; and

(b) even where traced through or to any person whose parents are not or have not been married to one another.

(3) For the avoidance of doubt sexual intercourse between persons who are not related to each other in a degree referred to in subsection (1) above is not incest.

Offensive weapons

47 Prohibition of the carrying of offensive weapons.

(1) Any person who [...] has with him in any public place any offensive weapon shall be guilty of an offence, and shall be liable—

(a) on summary conviction, to imprisonment for a term not exceeding six months or a fine not exceeding the statutory maximum, or both;

(b) on conviction on indictment, to imprisonment for a term not exceeding [5] years or a fine, or both.

[(1A) It is a defence for a person charged with an offence under subsection (1) to show that the person had a reasonable excuse or lawful authority for having the weapon with the person in the public place.

(2) Where any person is convicted of an offence under subsection (1) above the court may make an order for the forfeiture or disposal of any weapon in respect of which the offence was committed.

(3) [...]

[(4) In this section—

'offensive weapon' means any article—

(a) made or adapted for use for causing injury to a person, or

(b) intended, by the person having the article, for use for causing injury to a person by—

(i) the person having it, or

(ii) some other person,

'public place' means any place other than—

(a) domestic premises,

(b) school premises (within the meaning of section 49A(6)),

(c) a prison (within the meaning of section 49C(7)),

'domestic premises' means premises occupied as a private dwelling (including any stair, passage, garden, yard, garage, outhouse or other appurtenance of such premises which is not used in common by the occupants of more than one such dwelling).]

48 Search for offensive weapons.

(1) Where a constable has reasonable grounds for suspecting that any person is carrying an offensive weapon and has committed or is committing an offence under section 47 of this Act, the constable may search that person without warrant, and detain him for such time as is reasonably required to permit the search to be carried out; and he shall inform the person of the reason for such detention.

(2) Any person who—

(a) intentionally obstructs a constable in the exercise of the constable's powers under subsection (1) above; or

(b) conceals from a constable acting in the exercise of those powers an offensive weapon, shall be guilty of an offence and liable on summary conviction to a fine not exceeding level 4 on the standard scale.

(3) […]

(4) In this section, 'offensive weapon' has the same meaning as in the said section 47.

49 Offence of having in public place article with blade or point.

(1) Subject to subsections (4) and (5) below, any person who has an article to which this section applies with him in a public place shall be guilty of an offence and liable—

(a) on summary conviction, to imprisonment for a term not exceeding [twelve] months or a fine not exceeding the statutory maximum or both; and

(b) on conviction on indictment, to imprisonment for a term not exceeding [5] years or a fine or both.

(2) Subject to subsection (3) below, this section applies to any article which has a blade or is sharply pointed.

(3) This section does not apply to a folding pocketknife if the cutting edge of its blade does not exceed three inches (7.62 centimetres).

(4) It shall be a defence for a person charged with an offence under subsection (1) above to [show that the person had a reasonable excuse] or lawful authority for having the article with him in the public place.

(5) Without prejudice to the generality of subsection (4) above, it shall be a defence for a person charged with an offence under subsection (1) above to [show] that he had the article with him—

(a) for use at work;

(b) for religious reasons; or

(c) as part of any national costume.

(6) Where a person is convicted of an offence under subsection (1) above the court may make an order for the forfeiture of any article to which the offence relates, and any article forfeited under this subsection shall (subject to section 193 of the Criminal Procedure (Scotland) Act 1995 (suspension of

forfeiture etc, pending appeal)) be disposed of as the court may direct.

[(7) In this section, 'public place' has the same meaning as in section 47(4).]

Vandalism

52 Vandalism.

(1) Subject to subsection (2) below, any person who, without reasonable excuse, wilfully or recklessly destroys or damages any property belonging to another shall be guilty of the offence of vandalism.

(2) It shall not be competent to charge acts which constitute the offence of wilful fire-raising as vandalism under this section.

(3) Any person convicted of the offence of vandalism shall be liable on summary conviction—

(a) in the district court, to imprisonment for a term not exceeding 60 days, or to a fine not exceeding level 3 on the standard scale, or to both;

(b) in the sheriff court—

(i) for a first such offence, to imprisonment for a term not exceeding 3 months, or to a fine not exceeding the prescribed sum (within the meaning of section 225(8) of the Criminal Procedure (Scotland) Act 1995), or to both; and

(ii) for any subsequent such offence, to imprisonment for a term not exceeding 6 months, or to the fine mentioned in sub-paragraph (i) above, or to both.

CRIMINAL PROCEDURE (SCOTLAND) ACT 1995 (1995, c 46)

PART V
CHILDREN AND YOUNG PERSONS

[41 Age of criminal responsibility
A child under the age of 12 years cannot commit an offence.]

42 Prosecution of children.
(1) [A child aged 12 years or more but under 16 years may not] be prosecuted for any offence except on the instructions of the Lord Advocate, or at [the instance of the Lord Advocate]; and no court other than the High Court and the sheriff court shall have jurisdiction over [such a child] for an offence.

(2) Where a child is charged with any offence, his parent or guardian may in any case, and shall, if he can be found and resides within a reasonable distance, be required to attend at the court before which the case is heard or determined during all the stages of the proceedings, unless the court is satisfied that it would be unreasonable to require his attendance.

(3) […]

(4) For the purpose of enforcing the attendance of a parent or guardian and enabling him to take part in the proceedings and enabling orders to be made against him, rules may be made under section 305 of this Act, for applying, with the necessary adaptations and modifications, such of the provisions of this Act relating to summary proceedings as appear appropriate for the purpose.

(5) The parent or guardian whose attendance is required under this section is—

(a) the parent who has parental responsibilities or parental rights (within the meaning of sections 1(3) and 2(4) respectively of the Children (Scotland) Act 1995) in relation to the child; or

(b) the guardian having actual possession and control of him.

(6) The attendance of the parent of a child shall not be required under this section in any case where the child was before the institution of the proceedings removed from the care or charge of his parent by an order of a court.

(7) […]

(8) Where a local authority receive notification under [section 24 of the Criminal Justice (Scotland) Act 2016] they shall make such investigations and submit to the court a report which shall contain such information as to the home surroundings of the child as appear to them will assist the court in the disposal of his case, and the report shall contain information, which the appropriate education authority shall have a duty to supply, as to the school record, health and character of the child.

(9) Any child […] being conveyed to or from any criminal court, or waiting before or after attendance in such court, shall be prevented from associating with an adult (not being a relative) who is charged with any offence other than an offence with which the child is jointly charged.

(10) […]

PART VI
MENTAL DISORDER

[*Criminal responsibility of mentally disordered persons*

51A Criminal responsibility of persons with mental disorder

(1) A person is not criminally responsible for conduct constituting an offence, and is to be acquitted of the offence, if the person was at the time of the conduct unable by reason of mental disorder to appreciate the nature or wrongfulness of the conduct.

(2) But a person does not lack criminal responsibility for such conduct if the mental disorder in question consists only of a personality disorder which is characterised solely or principally by abnormally aggressive or seriously irresponsible conduct.

(3) The defence set out in subsection (1) is a special defence.

(4) The special defence may be stated only by the person charged with the offence and it is for that person to establish it on the balance of probabilities.

(5) In this section, 'conduct' includes acts and omissions.

Diminished responsibility

51B Diminished responsibility

(1) A person who would otherwise be convicted of murder is instead to be convicted of culpable homicide on grounds of diminished responsibility if the person's ability to determine or control conduct for which the person would otherwise be convicted of murder was, at the time of the conduct, substantially impaired by reason of abnormality of mind.

(2) For the avoidance of doubt, the reference in subsection (1) to abnormality of mind includes mental disorder.

(3) The fact that a person was under the influence of alcohol, drugs or any other substance at the time of the conduct in question does not of itself—

(a) constitute abnormality of mind for the purposes of subsection (1), or

(b) prevent such abnormality from being established for those purposes.

(4) It is for the person charged with murder to establish, on the balance of probabilities, that the condition set out in subsection (1) is satisfied.

(5) In this section, 'conduct' includes acts and omissions.]

[*Acquittal involving mental disorder*

53E Acquittal involving mental disorder

(1) Where the prosecutor accepts a plea (by the person charged with the commission of an offence) of the special defence set out in section 51A of this Act, the court must declare that the person is acquitted by reason of the special defence.

(2) Subsection (3) below applies where—

(a) the prosecutor does not accept such a plea, and

(b) evidence tending to establish the special defence set out in section 51A of this Act is brought before the court.

(3) Where this subsection applies the court is to—

(a) in proceedings on indictment, direct the jury to find whether the special defence has been established and, if they find that it has, to declare whether the person is acquitted on that ground,

(b) in summary proceedings, state whether the special defence has been established and, if it states that it has, declare whether the person is acquitted on that ground.]

[*Unfitness for trial*

53F Unfitness for trial

(1) A person is unfit for trial if it is established on the balance of probabilities that the person is incapable, by reason of a mental or physical condition, of participating effectively in a trial.

(2) In determining whether a person is unfit for trial the court is to have regard to—

(a) the ability of the person to—

(i) understand the nature of the charge,

(ii) understand the requirement to tender a plea to the charge and the effect of such a plea,

(iii) understand the purpose of, and follow the course of, the trial,

(iv) understand the evidence that may be given against the person,

(v) instruct and otherwise communicate with the person's legal representative, and

(b) any other factor which the court considers relevant.

(3) The court is not to find that a person is unfit for trial by reason only of the person being unable to recall whether the event which forms the basis of the charge occurred in the manner described in the charge.

(4) In this section 'the court' means—

(a) as regards a person charged on indictment, the High Court or the sheriff court,

(b) as regards a person charged summarily, the sheriff court.]

[…]

Examination of facts

55 Examination of facts.

(1) At an examination of facts ordered under section 54(1)(b) of this Act the court shall, on the basis of the evidence (if any) already given in the trial and such evidence, or further evidence, as may be led by either party, determine whether it is satisfied—

(a) beyond reasonable doubt, as respects any charge on the indictment or, as the case may be, the complaint in respect of which the accused was being or was to be tried, that he did the act or made the omission constituting the offence; and

(b) on the balance of probabilities, that there are no grounds for acquitting him.

(2) Where the court is satisfied as mentioned in subsection (1) above, it shall make a finding to that effect.

(3) Where the court is not so satisfied it shall, subject to subsection (4) below, acquit the person of the charge.

(4) Where, as respects a person acquitted under subsection (3) above, the court is satisfied as to the matter mentioned in subsection (1)(a) above but it appears to the court that the person was [not, because of section 51A of this Act, criminally responsible for the conduct] constituting the offence, the court shall state whether the acquittal is [by reason of the special defence set out in that section] .

(5) Where it appears to the court that it is not practical or appropriate for the accused to attend an examination of facts the court may, if no objection is taken by or on behalf of the accused, order that the examination of facts shall proceed in his absence.

(6) Subject to the provisions of this section, section 56 of this Act and any Act of Adjournal the rules of evidence and procedure and the powers of the court shall, in respect of an examination of facts, be as nearly as possible those applicable in respect of a trial.

(7) For the purposes of the application to an examination of facts of the rules and powers mentioned in subsection (6) above, an examination of facts—

(a) commences when the indictment or, as the case may be, complaint is called; and

(b) concludes when the court—

(i) acquits the person under subsection (3) above;

(ii) makes an order under subsection (2) of section 57 of this Act; or

(iii) decides, under paragraph (e) of that subsection, not to make an order.

56 Examination of facts: supplementary provisions.

(1) An examination of facts ordered under section 54(1)(b) of this Act may, where the order is made at the trial diet [or, in proceedings on indictment, at the first diet (in the case of proceedings in the sheriff court) or the preliminary hearing (in the case of proceedings in the High Court)] , be held immediately following the making of the order and, where it is so held, the citation of the accused and any witness to the trial diet [, first diet or, as the case may be, preliminary hearing] shall be a valid citation to the examination of facts.

(2) [...]

(3) Where an accused person is not legally represented at an examination of facts the court shall appoint counsel or a solicitor to represent his interests.

(4) The court may, on the motion of the prosecutor and after hearing the accused, order that the examination of facts shall proceed in relation to a particular charge, or particular charges, in the indictment or, as the case may be, complaint in priority to other such charges.

(5) The court may, on the motion of the prosecutor and after hearing the accused, at any time desert the examination of facts *pro loco et tempore* as respects either the whole indictment or, as the case may be, complaint or any charge therein.

(6) Where, and to the extent that, an examination of facts has, under subsection (5) above, been deserted *pro loco et tempore*—

(a) in the case of proceedings on indictment, the Lord Advocate may, at any time, raise and insist in a new indictment; or

(b) in the case of summary proceedings, the prosecutor may at any time raise a fresh libel,

notwithstanding any time limit which would otherwise apply in respect of prosecution of the alleged offence.

(7) If, in a case where a court has made a finding under subsection (2) of section 55 of this Act, a person is subsequently charged, whether on indictment or on a complaint, with an offence arising out of the same act or omission as is referred to in subsection (1) of that section, any order made under section 57(2) of this Act shall, with effect from the commencement of the later proceedings, cease to have effect.

(8) For the purposes of subsection (7) above, the later proceedings are commenced when the indictment or, as the case may be, the complaint is served.

Disposal [where accused found not criminally responsible]

57 Disposal of case where accused found [not criminally responsible or unfit for trial].

(1) This section applies where—

(a) a person is [acquitted by reason of the special defence set out in section 51A of this Act]; or

(b) following an examination of facts under section 55, a court makes a finding under subsection (2) of that section.

(2) Subject to subsection (3) below, where this section applies the court may, as it thinks fit—

(a) [subject to subsection (4) below, make a compulsion order [(whether or not authorising the detention of the person in a hospital)]];

[(b) subject to subsection (4A) below, make a restriction order in respect of the person (that is, in addition to a compulsion order authorising the detention of the person in a hospital);]

[[(bb) subject to subsections (3A) and (4B) below, make an interim compulsion order in respect of the person;]]

(c) [subject to subsections (4C) and (6) below, make a guardianship order in respect of the person];

(d) [subject to subsection (5) below,] make a supervision and treatment order (within the meaning of paragraph 1(1) of Schedule 4 to this Act [in respect of the person]); or

(e) make no order.

[(3) Where the court is satisfied, having regard to a report submitted in respect of the person following an interim [compulsion] order, that, on a balance of probabilities, the risk his being at liberty presents to the safety of the public at large is high, it shall make orders under both paragraphs (a) and (b) of subsection (2) above in respect of that person.]

[(3A) The court may make an interim compulsion order under paragraph (bb) of subsection (2) above in respect of a person only where it has not previously made such an order in respect of the person under that paragraph.]

[(4) For the purposes of subsection (2)(a) above—

(a) subsections (2) to (16) of section 57A of this Act shall apply as they apply for the purposes of subsection (1) of that section, subject to the following modifications—

(i) references to the offender shall be construed as references to the person to whom this section applies; and

(ii) in subsection (4)(b)(i), the reference to the offence of which the offender was convicted shall be construed as a reference to the offence with which the person to whom this section applies was charged;

(b) section 57B of this Act shall have effect subject to the modification that references to the offender shall be construed as references to the person to whom this section applies;

(c) section 57C of this Act shall have effect subject to the following modifications—

(i) references to the offender shall be construed as references to the person to whom this section applies; and

(ii) references to section 57A of this Act shall be construed as references to subsection (2)(a) above; and

(d) section 57D of this Act shall have effect subject to the modification that references to the offender shall be construed as references to the person to whom this section applies.

(4A) For the purposes of subsection (2)(b) above, section 59 of this Act shall have effect.

(4B) For the purposes of subsection (2)(bb) above—

(a) subsections (2) to (13) of section 53 of this Act shall apply as they apply for the purposes of subsection (1) of that section, subject to the following modifications—

(i) references to the offender shall be construed as references to the person to whom this section applies;

(ii) in subsection (3)(a)(ii), the reference to one of the disposals mentioned in subsection (6) of that section shall be construed as a reference to the disposal mentioned in subsection (6)(a) of that section;

(iii) in subsection (4)(a), the reference to the offence of which the offender is convicted shall be construed as a reference to the offence with which the person to whom this section applies is charged; and

(iv) subsection (6)(b) shall not apply;

(b) section 53A of this Act shall have effect subject to the modification that references to the offender shall be construed as references to the person to whom this section applies;

(c) section 53B of this Act shall have effect subject to the following modifications—

(i) references to the offender shall be construed as references to the person to whom this section applies; and

(ii) for paragraphs (a) and (b) of subsection (8) there shall be substituted ', revoke the interim compulsion order and—

(a) make an order in respect of the person under paragraph (a), (b), (c) or (d) of subsection (2) of section 57 of this Act; or

(b) decide, under paragraph (e) of that subsection, to make no order in respect of the person.';

(d) section 53C of this Act shall have effect subject to the following modifications—

(i) references to the offender shall be construed as references to the person to whom this section applies; and

(ii) for paragraphs (a) to (c) of subsection (1) there shall be substituted—

'(a) makes an order in respect of the person under paragraph (a), (b), (c) or (d) of subsection (2) of section 57 of this Act; or

(b) decides, under paragraph (e) of that subsection, to make no order in respect of the person.'; and

(e) section 53D of this Act shall have effect subject to the modification that the reference to the offender shall be construed as a reference to the person to whom this section applies.

(4C) For the purposes of subsection (2)(c) above, subsections (1A), (6) to (8) and (11) of section 58 of this Act shall apply, subject to the modifications that the reference to a person convicted and any references to the offender shall be construed as references to the person to whom this section applies.]

(5) Schedule 4 to this Act shall have effect as regards supervision and treatment orders.

[(6) Section 58A of this Act shall have effect as regards guardianship orders made under subsection (2)(c) of this section.]

[70A Defence statements

(1) This section applies where an indictment is served on an accused.

(2) The accused must lodge a defence statement at least 14 days before the first diet.

(3) The accused must lodge a defence statement at least 14 days before the preliminary hearing.

(4) At least 7 days before the trial diet the accused must—

(a) where there has been no material change in circumstances in relation to the accused's defence since the last defence statement was lodged, lodge a statement stating that fact,

(b) where there has been a material change in circumstances in relation to the accused's defence since the last defence statement was lodged, lodge a defence statement.

(5) If after lodging a statement under subsection (2), (3) or (4) there is a material change in circumstances in relation to the accused's defence, the accused must lodge a defence statement.

(6) Where subsection (5) requires a defence statement to be lodged, it must be lodged before the trial diet begins unless on cause shown the court allows it to be lodged during the trial diet.

(7) The accused may lodge a defence statement—

(a) at any time before the trial diet, or

(b) during the trial diet if the court on cause shown allows it.

(8) As soon as practicable after lodging a defence statement or a statement under subsection (4)(a), the accused must send a copy of the statement to the prosecutor and any co-accused.

(9) In this section, 'defence statement' means a statement setting out—

(a) the nature of the accused's defence, including any particular defences on which the accused intends to rely,

(b) any matters of fact on which the accused takes issue with the prosecution and the reason for doing so,

(c) particulars of the matters of fact on which the accused intends to rely for the purposes of the accused's defence,

(d) any point of law which the accused wishes to take and any authority on which the accused intends to rely for that purpose,

(e) by reference to the accused's defence, the nature of any information that the accused requires the prosecutor to disclose, and

(f) the reasons why the accused considers that disclosure by the prosecutor of any such information is necessary.]

Notice by accused

78 Special defences, incrimination and notice of witnesses, etc.

(1) It shall not be competent for an accused to state a special defence or to lead evidence calculated to exculpate the accused by incriminating a co-accused unless—

(a) a plea of special defence or, as the case may be, notice of intention to lead such evidence has been lodged and intimated in writing in accordance with subsection (3) below [...]

(b) the court, on cause shown, otherwise directs.

[(1A) Subsection (1) does not apply where—

(a) the accused lodges a defence statement under section 70A, and

(b) the accused's defence consists of or includes a special defence.]

(2) Subsection (1) above shall apply [to a plea of diminished responsibility or] to a defence of automatism [, coercion or, in a prosecution for an offence to which section 288C of this Act applies, consent] as if it were a special defence.

[(2A) In subsection (2) above, the reference to a defence of consent is a reference to the defence which is stated by reference to the complainer's consent to the act which is the subject matter of the charge or the accused's belief as to that consent.

(2B) In subsection (2A) above, 'complainer' has the same meaning as in section 274 of this Act.]

(3) A plea or notice is lodged and intimated in accordance with this subsection—

(a) where [the case is to be tried in the High Court], by lodging the plea or notice with the Clerk of Justiciary and by intimating the plea or notice to the Crown Agent and to any co-accused not less than [seven clear days before the preliminary hearing];

(b) where the [case is to be tried in the sheriff court], by lodging the plea or notice with the sheriff clerk and by intimating it to the procurator fiscal and to any co-accused at or before the first diet.

(4) It shall not be competent for the accused to examine any witnesses or to put in evidence any productions not included in the lists lodged by the prosecutor unless—

(a) written notice of the names and addresses of such witnesses and of such productions has been given—

(i) where the case is to be tried in the sheriff court, to the procurator fiscal of the district of the trial diet at or before the first diet; and

(ii) where the case is to be tried in the High Court, to the Crown Agent at least [seven clear days before the preliminary hearing]

(b) the court, on cause shown, otherwise directs.

(5) A copy of every written notice required by subsection (4) above shall be lodged by the accused with the sheriff clerk of the district in which the trial diet is to be held, or in any case the trial diet of which is to be held in the High Court in Edinburgh with the Clerk of Justiciary, at or before

[(a) where the case is to be tried in the High Court, the preliminary hearing;

(b) where the case is to be tried in the sheriff court, the trial diet,

for the use of the court.].

101 Previous convictions: solemn proceedings.

(1) Previous convictions against the accused shall not [, subject to subsection (2) below and section 275A(2) of this Act,] be laid before the jury, nor shall reference be made to them in presence of the jury before the verdict is returned.

(2) Nothing in subsection (1) above shall prevent the prosecutor—

(a) asking the accused questions tending to show that he has been convicted of an offence other than that with which he is charged, where he is entitled to do so under section 266 of this Act; or

(b) leading evidence of previous convictions where it is competent to do so under section 270 of this Act,

and nothing in this section or in section 69 of this Act shall prevent evidence of previous convictions being led in any case where such evidence is competent in support of a substantive charge.

(3) Previous convictions shall not [, subject to section 275A(1) of this Act,] be laid before the presiding judge until the prosecutor moves

[(a)] for sentence [; or]

[(b) for a risk assessment order (or the court at its own instance proposes to make such an order)],

and in that event the prosecutor shall lay before the judge a copy of the notice referred to in subsection (2) or (4) of section 69 of this Act.

[(3A) Where, under paragraph (b) of subsection (3) above, the prosecutor lays previous convictions before the judge, he shall also provide the judge with such details regarding the offences in question as are available to him.]

(4) On the conviction of the accused it shall be competent for the court, subject to subsection (5) below, to amend a notice of previous convictions so laid by deletion or alteration for the purpose of curing any error or defect.

(5) […]

(6) Any conviction which is admitted in evidence by the court shall be entered in the record of the trial.

(7) Where a person is convicted of an offence, the court may have regard to any previous conviction in respect of that person in deciding on the disposal of the case.

(8) Where any such intimation as is mentioned in section 69 of this Act is given by the accused, it shall be competent to prove any previous conviction included in a notice under that section in the manner specified in section 285 [, or as the

case may be 286A,] of this Act, and the provisions of the [section in question] shall apply accordingly.

[(9) This section, except subsection (2) above, applies in relation to the alternative disposals mentioned in subsection (10) below as it applies in relation to previous convictions.

(10) Those alternative disposals are—

(a) a—

(i) fixed penalty under section 302(1) of this Act;

(ii) compensation offer under section 302A(1) of this Act,

that has been accepted (or deemed to have been accepted) by the accused in the two years preceding the date of an offence charged;

(b) a work order under section 303ZA(6) of this Act that has been completed in the two years preceding the date of an offence charged[;

(c) a restoration notice given under subsection (4) of section 20A of the Nature Conservation (Scotland) Act 2004 (asp 6) in respect of which the accused has given notice of intention to comply under subsection (5) of that section in the two years preceding the date of an offence charged.]

(11) Nothing in this section or in section 69 of this Act shall prevent the prosecutor, following conviction of an accused of an offence—

(a) to which a fixed penalty offer made under section 302(1) of this Act related;

(b) to which a compensation offer made under section 302A(1) of this Act related; ...

(c) to which a work offer made under section 303ZA(1) of this Act related[; or

(d) to which a restoration notice given under section 20A(4) of the Nature Conservation (Scotland) Act 2004 (asp 6) related,]

providing the judge with information about the making of the offer (including the terms of the offer) [or, as the case may be, about the giving of the notice (including the terms of the notice).]]

[(12) Any reference in this section to a previous conviction includes, where relevant, a conviction by a court in any part of the United Kingdom or in any member State of the European Union.]

Hearsay

259 Exceptions to the rule that hearsay evidence is inadmissible.

(1) Subject to the following provisions of this section, evidence of a statement made by a person otherwise than while giving oral evidence in court in criminal proceedings shall be admissible in those proceedings as evidence of any matter contained in the statement where the judge is satisfied—

(a) that the person who made the statement will not give evidence in the proceedings of such matter for any of the reasons mentioned in subsection (2) below;

(b) that evidence of the matter would be admissible in the proceedings if that person gave direct oral evidence of it;

(c) that the person who made the statement would have been, at the time the statement was made, a competent witness in such proceedings; and

(d) that there is evidence which would entitle a jury properly directed, or in summary proceedings would entitle the judge, to find that the statement was made and that either—

(i) it is contained in a document; or

(ii) a person who gave oral evidence in the proceedings as to the statement has direct personal knowledge of the making of the statement.

(2) The reasons referred to in paragraph (a) of subsection (1) above are that the person who made the statement—

(a) is dead or is, by reason of his bodily or mental condition, unfit or unable to give evidence in any competent manner;

(b) is named and otherwise sufficiently identified, but is out with the United Kingdom and it is not reasonably practicable to secure his attendance at the trial or to obtain his evidence in any other competent manner;

(c) is named and otherwise sufficiently identified, but cannot be found and all reasonable steps which, in the circumstances, could have been taken to find him have been so taken;

(d) having been authorised to do so by virtue of a ruling of the court in the proceedings that he is entitled to refuse to give evidence in connection with the subject matter of the statement on the grounds that such evidence might incriminate him, refuses to give such evidence; or

(e) is called as a witness and either—

(i) refuses to take the oath or affirmation; or

(ii) having been sworn as a witness and directed by the judge to give evidence in connection with the subject matter of the statement refuses to do so,

and in the application of this paragraph to a child, the reference to a witness refusing to take the oath or affirmation or, as the case may be, to having been sworn shall be construed as a reference to a child who has refused to accept an admonition to tell the truth or, having been so admonished, refuses to give evidence as mentioned above.

(3) Evidence of a statement shall not be admissible by virtue of subsection (1) above where the judge is satisfied that the occurrence of any of the circumstances mentioned in paragraphs (a) to (e) of subsection (2) above, by virtue of which the statement would otherwise be admissible, is caused by—

(a) the person in support of whose case the evidence would be given; or

(b) any other person acting on his behalf,

for the purpose of securing that the person who made the statement does not give evidence for the purposes of the proceedings either at all or in connection with the subject matter of the statement.

(4) Where in any proceedings evidence of a statement made by any person is admitted by reference to any of the reasons mentioned in paragraphs (a) to (c) and (e)(i) of subsection (2) above—

(a) any evidence which, if that person had given evidence in connection with the subject matter of the statement, would have been admissible as relevant to his credibility as a witness shall be admissible for that purpose in those proceedings;

(b) evidence may be given of any matter which, if that person had given evidence in connection with the subject matter of the statement, could have been put to him in cross-examination as relevant to his credibility as a witness but of which evidence could not have been adduced by the cross-examining party; and

(c) evidence tending to prove that that person, whether before or after making the statement, made in whatever manner some other statement which is inconsistent with it shall be admissible for the purpose of showing that he has contradicted himself.

(5) Subject to subsection (6) below, where a party intends to apply to have evidence of a statement admitted by virtue of subsection (1) above he shall, [by the relevant time], give notice in writing of—

(a) that fact;

(b) the witnesses and productions to be adduced in connection with such evidence; and

(c) such other matters as may be prescribed by Act of Adjournal,

to every other party to the proceedings and, for the purposes of this subsection, such evidence may be led notwithstanding that a witness or production concerned is not included in any list lodged by the parties and that the notice required by sections 67(5) and 78(4) of this Act has not been given.

[(5A) In subsection (5) above, 'the relevant time' means—

(a) in the case of proceedings in the High Court—

(i) not less than 7 days before the preliminary hearing; or

(ii) such later time, before the trial diet, as the judge may on cause shown allow;

(b) in any other case, before the trial diet.]

(6) A party shall not be required to give notice as mentioned in subsection (5) above where—

(a) the grounds for seeking to have evidence of a statement admitted are as mentioned in paragraph (d) or (e) of subsection (2) above; or

(b) he satisfies the judge that there was good reason for not giving such notice.

(7) If no other party to the proceedings objects to the admission of evidence of a statement by virtue of subsection (1) above, the evidence shall be admitted without the judge requiring to be satisfied as mentioned in that subsection.

(8) For the purposes of the determination of any matter upon which the judge is required to be satisfied under subsection (1) above—

(a) except to the extent that any other party to the proceedings challenges them and insists in such challenge, it shall be presumed that the circumstances are as stated by the party seeking to introduce evidence of the statement; and

(b) where such a challenge is insisted in, the judge shall determine the matter on the balance of probabilities, and he may draw any reasonable inference—

(i) from the circumstances in which the statement was made or otherwise came into being; or

(ii) from any other circumstances, including, where the statement is contained in a document, the form and contents of the document.

(9) Where evidence of a statement has been admitted by virtue of subsection (1) above on the application of one party to the proceedings, without prejudice to anything in any enactment or rule of law, the judge may permit any party to lead additional evidence of such description as the judge may specify, notwithstanding that a witness or production concerned is not included in any list lodged by the parties and that the notice required by sections 67(5) and 78(4) of this Act has not been given.

(10) Any reference in subsections (5), (6) and (9) above to evidence shall include a reference to evidence led in connection with any determination required to be made for the purposes of subsection (1) above.

260 Admissibility of prior statements of witnesses.

(1) Subject to the following provisions of this section, where a witness gives evidence in criminal proceedings, any prior statement made by the witness shall be admissible as evidence of any matter stated in it of which direct oral evidence by him would be admissible if given in the course of those proceedings.

(2) A prior statement shall not be admissible under this section unless—

(a) the statement is contained in a document;

(b) the witness, in the course of giving evidence, indicates that the statement was made by him and that he adopts it as his evidence; and

(c) at the time the statement was made, the person who made it would have been a competent witness in the proceedings.

(3) For the purposes of this section, any reference to a prior statement is a reference to a prior statement which, but for the provisions of this section, would not be admissible as evidence of any matter stated in it.

(4) Subsections (2) and (3) above do not apply to a prior statement—

(a) contained in a precognition on oath; or

(b) made in other proceedings, whether criminal or civil and whether taking place in the United Kingdom or elsewhere,

and, for the purposes of this section, any such statement shall not be admissible unless it is sufficiently authenticated.

[(5) A prior statement made by a witness shall not, in any proceedings on indictment, be inadmissible by reason only that it is not included in any list of productions lodged by the parties.]

261 [Statements by co-accused]

(1) Subject to the following provisions of this section, nothing in sections 259 and 260 of this Act shall apply to a statement made by the accused.

(2) Evidence of a statement made by an accused shall be admissible by virtue of the said section 259 at the instance of another accused in the same proceedings as evidence in relation to that other accused.

(3) For the purposes of subsection (2) above, the first mentioned accused shall be deemed—

(a) where he does not give evidence in the proceedings, to be a witness refusing to give evidence in connection with the subject matter of the statement as mentioned in paragraph (e) of subsection (2) of the said section 259; and

(b) to have been, at the time the statement was made, a competent witness in the proceedings.

(4) Evidence of a statement shall not be admissible as mentioned in subsection (2) above unless the accused at whose instance it is sought to be admitted has given notice of his intention to do so as mentioned in subsection (5) of the said section 259; but subsection (6) of that section shall not apply in the case of notice required to be given by virtue of this subsection.

[261ZA Statements by accused

(1) Evidence of a statement to which this subsection applies is not inadmissible as evidence of any fact contained in the statement on account of the evidence's being hearsay.

(2) Subsection (1) applies to a statement made by the accused in the course of the accused's being questioned (whether as a suspect or not) by a constable, or another official, investigating an offence.

(3) Subsection (1) does not affect the issue of whether evidence of a statement made by one accused is admissible as evidence in relation to another accused.]

Witnesses

263 Examination of witnesses.

(1) In any trial, it shall be competent for the party against whom a witness is produced and sworn *in causa* to examine such witness both in cross and *in causa*.

(2) The judge may, on the motion of either party, on cause shown order that the examination of a witness for that party ('the first witness') shall be interrupted to permit the examination of another witness for that party.

(3) Where the judge makes an order under subsection (2) above he shall, after the examination of the other witness, permit the recall of the first witness.

(4) In a trial, a witness may be examined as to whether he has on any specified occasion made a statement on any matter pertinent to the issue at the trial different from the evidence given by him in the trial; and evidence may be led in the trial to prove that the witness made the different statement on the occasion specified.

(5) In any trial, on the motion of either party, the presiding judge may permit a witness who has been examined to be recalled.

[264 Spouse or civil partner of accused a compellable witness

(1) The spouse or civil partner of an accused is a competent and compellable witness for the prosecution, the accused or any co-accused in the proceedings against the accused.

(2) Subsection (1) is, if the spouse or civil partner is a co-accused in the proceedings, subject to any enactment or rule of law by virtue of which an accused need not (by reason of being an accused) give evidence in the proceedings.

(3) Subsection (1) displaces any other rule of law that would (but for that subsection) prevent or restrict, by reference to the relationship, the giving of evidence by the spouse or civil partner of an accused.]

266 Accused as witness.

(1) Subject to subsections (2) to (8) below, the accused shall be a competent witness for the defence at every stage of the case, whether the accused is on trial alone or along with a co-accused.

(2) The accused shall not be called as a witness in pursuance of this section except upon his own application or in accordance with subsection (9) or (10) below.

(3) An accused who gives evidence on his own behalf in pursuance of this section may be asked any question in cross-examination notwithstanding that it would tend to incriminate him as to the offence charged.

(4) An accused who gives evidence on his own behalf in pursuance of this section shall not be asked, and if asked shall not be required to answer, any question tending to show that he has committed, or been convicted of, or been charged with, any offence other than that with which he is then charged, or is of bad character, unless—

(a) the proof that he has committed or been convicted of such other offence is admissible evidence to show that he is guilty of the offence with which he is then charged; or

(b) the accused or his counsel or solicitor has asked questions of the witnesses for the prosecution with a view to establishing the accused's good character or impugning the character of the complainer, or the accused has given evidence of his own good character, or the nature or conduct of the defence is such as to involve imputations on the character of the prosecutor or of the witnesses for the prosecution or of the complainer; or

(c) the accused has given evidence against any other person charged in the same proceedings.

(5) In a case to which paragraph (b) of subsection (4) above applies, the prosecutor shall be entitled to ask the accused a question of a kind specified in that subsection only if the court, on the application of the prosecutor, permits him to do so.

[(5A) Nothing in subsections (4) and (5) above shall prevent the accused from being asked, or from being required to answer, any question tending to show that he has been convicted of an offence other than that with which he is charged if his conviction for that other offence has been disclosed to the jury, or is to be taken into consideration by the judge, under section 275A(2) of this Act.]

(6) An application under subsection (5) above in proceedings on indictment shall be made in the course of the trial but in the absence of the jury.

(7) In subsection (4) above, references to the complainer include references to a victim who is deceased.

(8) Every person called as a witness in pursuance of this section shall, unless otherwise ordered by the court, give his evidence from the witness box or other place from which the other witnesses give their evidence.

(9) The accused may—

(a) with the consent of a co-accused, call that other accused as a witness on the accused's behalf; or

(b) ask a co-accused any question in cross-examination if that co-accused gives evidence,

but he may not do both in relation to the same co-accused.

(10) The prosecutor or the accused may call as a witness a co-accused who has pleaded guilty to or been acquitted of all charges against him which remain before the court (whether or not, in a case where the co-accused has pleaded guilty to any charge, he has been sentenced) or in respect of whom the diet has been deserted; and the party calling such co-accused as a witness shall not require to give notice thereof, but the court may grant any other party such adjournment or postponement of the trial as may seem just.

(11) Where, in any trial, the accused is to be called as a witness he shall be so called as the first witness for the defence unless the court, on cause shown, otherwise directs.

267 Witnesses in court during trial.

(1) The court may, on an application by any party to the proceedings, permit a witness to be in court during the proceedings or any part of the proceedings before he has given evidence if it appears to the court that the presence of the witness would not be contrary to the interests of justice.

(2) Without prejudice to subsection (1) above, where a witness has, without the permission of the court and without the consent of the parties to the proceedings, been present in court during the proceedings, the court may, in its discretion, admit the witness, where it appears to the court that the presence of the witness was not the result of culpable negligence or criminal intent, and that the witness has not been unduly instructed or influenced by what took place during his presence, or that injustice will not be done by his examination.

270 Evidence of criminal record and character of accused.

(1) This section applies where—

(a) evidence is led by the defence, or the defence asks questions of a witness for the prosecution, with a view to establishing the accused's good character or impugning the character of the prosecutor, of any witness for the prosecution or of the complainer; or

(b) the nature or conduct of the defence is such as to tend to establish the accused's good character or to involve imputations on the character of the prosecutor, of any witness for the prosecution or of the complainer.

(2) Where this section applies the court may, without prejudice to section 268 of this Act, on the application of the prosecutor, permit the prosecutor to lead evidence that the accused has committed, or has been convicted of, or has been charged with, offences other than that for which he is being tried, or is of bad character, notwithstanding that, in proceedings on indictment, a witness or production concerned is not included in any list lodged by the prosecutor and that the notice required by sections 67(5) and 78(4) of this Act has not been given.

(3) In proceedings on indictment, an application under subsection (2) above shall be made in the course of the trial but in the absence of the jury.

(4) In subsection (1) above, references to the complainer include references to a victim who is deceased.

Evidence relating to sexual offences

[274 Restrictions on evidence relating to sexual offences.

(1) In the trial of a person charged with an offence to which section 288C of this Act applies, the court shall not admit, or allow questioning designed to elicit, evidence which shows or tends to show that the complainer—

(a) is not of good character (whether in relation to sexual matters or otherwise);

(b) has, at any time, engaged in sexual behaviour not forming part of the subject matter of the charge;

(c) has, at any time (other than shortly before, at the same time as or shortly after the acts which form part of the subject matter of the charge), engaged in such behaviour, not being sexual behaviour, as might found the inference that the complainer—

(i) is likely to have consented to those acts; or

(ii) is not a credible or reliable witness; or

(d) has, at any time, been subject to any such condition or predisposition as might found the inference referred to in sub-paragraph (c) above.

(2) In subsection (1) above—

'complainer' means the person against whom the offence referred to in that subsection is alleged to have been committed; and

the reference to engaging in sexual behaviour includes a reference to undergoing or being made subject to any experience of a sexual nature.]

[275 Exceptions to restrictions under section 274.

(1) The court may, on application made to it, admit such evidence or allow such questioning as is referred to in subsection (1) of section 274 of this Act if satisfied that—

(a) the evidence or questioning will relate only to a specific occurrence or occurrences of sexual or other behaviour or to specific facts demonstrating—

(i) the complainer's character; or

(ii) any condition or predisposition to which the complainer is or has been subject;

(b) that occurrence or those occurrences of behaviour or facts are relevant to establishing whether the accused is guilty of the offence with which he is charged; and

(c) the probative value of the evidence sought to be admitted or elicited is significant and is likely to outweigh any risk of prejudice to the proper administration of justice arising from its being admitted or elicited.

(2) In subsection (1) above—

(a) the reference to an occurrence or occurrences of sexual behaviour includes a reference to undergoing or being made subject to any experience of a sexual nature;

(b) 'the proper administration of justice' includes—

(i) appropriate protection of a complainer's dignity and privacy; and

(ii) ensuring that the facts and circumstances of which a jury is made aware are, in cases of offences to which section 288C of this Act applies, relevant to an issue which is to be put before the jury and commensurate to the importance of that issue to the jury's verdict,

and, in that subsection and in sub-paragraph (i) of paragraph (b) above, 'complainer' has the same meaning as in section 274 of this Act.

(3) An application for the purposes of subsection (1) above shall be in writing and shall set out—

(a) the evidence sought to be admitted or elicited;

(b) the nature of any questioning proposed;

(c) the issues at the trial to which that evidence is considered to be relevant;

(d) the reasons why that evidence is considered relevant to those issues;

(e) the inferences which the applicant proposes to submit to the court that it should draw from that evidence; and

(f) such other information as is of a kind specified for the purposes of this paragraph in Act of Adjournal.

(4) The party making such an application shall, when making it, send a copy of it—

(a) when that party is the prosecutor, to the accused; and

(b) when that party is the accused, to the prosecutor and any co-accused.

(5) The court may reach a decision under subsection (1) above without considering any evidence; but, where it takes evidence for the purposes of reaching that decision, it shall do so as if determining the admissibility of evidence.

(6) The court shall state its reasons for its decision under subsection (1) above, and may make that decision subject to conditions which may include compliance with directions issued by it.

(7) Where a court admits evidence or allows questioning under subsection (1) above, its decision to do so shall include a statement—

(a) of what items of evidence it is admitting or lines of questioning it is allowing;

(b) of the reasons for its conclusion that the evidence to be admitted or to be elicited by the questioning is admissible;

(c) of the issues at the trial to which it considers that that evidence is relevant.

(8) A condition under subsection (6) above may consist of a limitation on the extent to which evidence—

(a) to be admitted; or

(b) to be elicited by questioning to be allowed,

may be argued to support a particular inference specified in the condition.

(9) Where evidence is admitted or questioning allowed under this section, the court at any time may—

(a) as it thinks fit; and

(b) notwithstanding the terms of its decision under subsection (1) above or any condition under subsection (6) above, limit the extent of evidence to be admitted or questioning to be allowed.]

[275A Disclosure of accused's previous convictions where court allows questioning or evidence under section 275

(1) Where, under section 275 of this Act, a court [(or, in proceedings before a commissioner appointed under section 271I(1) or by virtue of section 272(1)(b) of this Act, a commissioner)] on the application of the accused allows such questioning or admits such evidence as is referred to in section 274(1) of this Act, the prosecutor shall forthwith place before the presiding judge any previous relevant conviction of the accused.

(2) [Subject to subsection (2A) any] conviction placed before the judge under subsection (1) above shall, unless the accused objects, be—

(a) in proceedings on indictment, laid before the jury;

(b) in summary proceedings, taken into consideration by the judge.

[(2A) Where the conviction is a relevant conviction by virtue of subsection (10)(aa)(ii), subsection (2) applies only if the judge considers it appropriate.]

(3) An extract of [a conviction referred to in subsection (2)] may not be laid before the jury or taken into consideration by the judge unless such an extract was appended to the notice, served on the accused under section 69(2) or, as the case may be, 166(2) of this Act, which specified that conviction.

(4) An objection under subsection (2) above may be made only on one or more of the following grounds—

(a) where the conviction bears to be a relevant conviction by virtue only of paragraph (b) of subsection (10) below, that there was not a substantial sexual element present in the commission of the offence for which the accused has been convicted;

(b) that the disclosure or, as the case may be, the taking into consideration of the conviction would be contrary to the interests of justice;

(c) in proceedings on indictment, that the conviction does not apply to the accused or is otherwise inadmissible;

(d) in summary proceedings, that the accused does not admit the conviction.

(5) Where—

(a) an objection is made on one or more of the grounds mentioned in paragraphs (b) to (d) of subsection (4) above; and

(b) an extract of the conviction in respect of which the objection is made was not appended to the notice, served on the accused under section 69(2) or, as the case may be, 166(2) above, which specified that conviction,

the prosecutor may, notwithstanding subsection (3) above, place such an extract conviction before the judge.

(6) In summary proceedings, the judge may, notwithstanding subsection (2)(b) above, take into consideration any extract placed before him under subsection (5) above for the purposes only of considering the objection in respect of which the extract is disclosed.

(7) In entertaining an objection on the ground mentioned in paragraph (b) of subsection (4) above, the court shall, unless the contrary is shown, presume that the disclosure, or, as the case may be, the taking into consideration, of a conviction is in the interests of justice.

(8) An objection on the ground mentioned in paragraph (c) of subsection (4) above shall not be entertained unless the accused has, under subsection (2) of section 69 of this Act, given intimation of the objection in accordance with subsection (3) of that section.

(9) In entertaining an objection on the ground mentioned in paragraph (d) of subsection (4) above, the court shall require the prosecutor to withdraw the conviction or adduce evidence in proof thereof.

(10) For the purposes of this section a 'relevant conviction' is, subject to subsection (11) below—

(a) a conviction for an offence to which section 288C of this Act applies by virtue of subsection (2) thereof; [...]

[(aa) a conviction by a court in—

(i) England and Wales or Northern Ireland, or

(ii) a member State of the European Union,

of an offence that is equivalent to one to which section 288C of this Act applies by virtue of subsection (2) thereof, or]

(b) where a substantial sexual element was present in the commission of any other offence in respect of which the accused has previously been convicted, a conviction for that offence,

which is specified in a notice served on the accused under section 69(2) or, as the case may be, 166(2) of this Act.

[(10A) Any issue of equivalence arising in pursuance of subsection (10)(aa) is for the court to determine.]

(11) A conviction for an offence other than an offence to which section 288C of this Act applies by virtue of subsection (2) thereof is not a relevant conviction for the purposes of this section unless an extract of that conviction containing information which indicates that a sexual element was present in the commission of the offence was appended to the notice, served on the accused under section 69(2) or, as the case may be, 166(2) of this Act, which specified that conviction.

[*Expert evidence as to subsequent behaviour of complainer*

275C Expert evidence as to subsequent behaviour of complainer in certain cases

(1) This section applies in the case of proceedings in respect of any—

[(a)] offence to which section 288C of this Act applies,

[(b) an offence under section 1(1) of the Domestic Abuse (Scotland) Act 2018,

(c) an offence that is aggravated as described in section 1(1)(a) of the Abusive Behaviour and Sexual Harm (Scotland) Act 2016.]

(2) Expert psychological or psychiatric evidence relating to any subsequent behaviour or statement of the complainer is admissible for the purpose of rebutting any inference adverse to the complainer's credibility or reliability as a witness which might otherwise be drawn from the behaviour or statement.

(3) In subsection (2) above—

'complainer' means the person against whom the offence to which the proceedings relate is alleged to have been committed,

'subsequent behaviour or statement' means any behaviour or statement subsequent to, and not forming part of the acts constituting, the offence to which the proceedings relate and which is not otherwise relevant to any fact in issue at the trial.

[(3A) Where the offence is as referred to in subsection (1)(b) above, the reference in the last definition in subsection (3) above to any behaviour or statement subsequent to the offence includes any behaviour or statement subsequent to a particular part of the course of behaviour of which the offence consists.]

(4) This section does not affect the admissibility of any evidence which is admissible otherwise than by virtue of this section.]

[*Dockets and charges in sex cases*

288BA Dockets for charges of sexual offences

(1) An indictment or a complaint may include a docket which specifies any act or omission that is connected with a sexual offence charged in the indictment or complaint.

(2) Here, an act or omission is connected with such an offence charged if it—

(a) is specifiable by way of reference to a sexual offence, and

(b) relates to—

(i) the same event as the offence charged, or

(ii) a series of events of which that offence is also part.

(3) The docket is to be in the form of a note apart from the offence charged.

(4) It does not matter whether the act or omission, if it were instead charged as an offence, could not competently be dealt with by the court (including as particularly constituted) in which the indictment or complaint is proceeding.

(5) Where under subsection (1) a docket is included in an indictment or a complaint, it is to be presumed that—

(a) the accused person has been given fair notice of the prosecutor's intention to lead evidence of the act or omission specified in the docket, and

(b) evidence of the act or omission is admissible as relevant.

(6) The references in this section to a sexual offence are to—

(a) an offence under the Sexual Offences (Scotland) Act 2009,

(b) any other offence involving a significant sexual element.

293 Statutory offences: art and part and aiding and abetting.

(1) A person may be convicted of, and punished for, a contravention of any enactment, notwithstanding that he was guilty of such contravention as art and part only.

(2) Without prejudice to subsection (1) above or to any express provision in any enactment having the like effect to this subsection, any person who aids, abets, counsels, procures or incites any other person to commit an offence against the provisions of any enactment shall be guilty of an offence and shall be liable on conviction, unless the enactment otherwise requires, to the same punishment as might be imposed on conviction of the first-mentioned offence.

294 Attempt at crime.

(1) Attempt to commit any indictable crime is itself an indictable crime.

(2) Attempt to commit any offence punishable on complaint shall itself be an offence punishable on complaint.

COMMUNICATIONS ACT 2003
(2003, c 21)

127 Improper use of public electronic communications network

(1) A person is guilty of an offence if he—

(a) sends by means of a public electronic communications network a message or other matter that is grossly offensive or of an indecent, obscene or menacing character; or

(b) causes any such message or matter to be so sent.

(2) A person is guilty of an offence if, for the purpose of causing annoyance, inconvenience or needless anxiety to another, he—

[(a) sends by means of a public electronic communications network, a message that he knows to be false,]

[(b) causes such a message to be sent; or]

(c) persistently makes use of a public electronic communications network.

(3) A person guilty of an offence under this section shall be liable, on summary conviction, to imprisonment for a term not exceeding six months or to a fine not exceeding level 5 on the standard scale, or to both.

(4) Subsections (1) and (2) do not apply to anything done in the course of providing a programme service (within the meaning of the Broadcasting Act 1990 (c. 42)).

[(5) An information or complaint relating to an offence under this section may be tried by a magistrates' court in England and Wales or Northern Ireland if it is laid or made—

(a) before the end of the period of 3 years beginning with the day on which the offence was committed, and

(b) before the end of the period of 6 months beginning with the day on which evidence comes to the knowledge of the prosecutor which the prosecutor considers sufficient to justify proceedings.

(6) Summary proceedings for an offence under this section may be commenced in Scotland—

(a) before the end of the period of 3 years beginning with the day on which the offence was committed, and

(b) before the end of the period of 6 months beginning with the day on which evidence comes to the knowledge of the prosecutor which the prosecutor considers sufficient to justify proceedings,

and section 136(3) of the Criminal Procedure (Scotland) Act 1995 (date when proceedings deemed to be commenced) applies for the purposes of this subsection as it applies for the purposes of that section.

(7) A certificate of a prosecutor as to the date on which evidence described in subsection (5)(b) or (6)(b) came to his or her knowledge is conclusive evidence of that fact.]

EMERGENCY WORKERS (SCOTLAND) ACT 2005
(2005, asp 2)

1 Assaulting or impeding certain providers of emergency services

(1) A person who assaults, obstructs or hinders another person acting in a capacity mentioned in subsection (3) below commits an offence.

(2) No offence is committed under subsection (1) above unless the person who assaults, obstructs or hinders knows or ought to know that the person being assaulted, obstructed or hindered is acting in that capacity.

(3) The capacity referred to in subsection (1) above is—

(a) that of a constable;

[(zb) that of a person employed by [the Scottish Fire and Rescue Service while discharging any of the Service's functions] under any of sections 9 to 13 (fire-fighting, road traffic accidents, other emergencies, emergency directions and other eventualities), 25, 27 and 29 (powers of authorised employees in relation to emergencies, obtaining information and investigating fires) of that Act;

(b) that of a person providing assistance under arrangements made by virtue of section 35 (assistance other than from relevant authorities) or 36 (arrangements for carrying out of functions by others) of the Fire (Scotland) Act 2005 other than assistance given to [the Scottish Fire and Rescue Service for the purpose of carrying out any of the functions conferred on the Service] by section 8 or 61 of that Act;] [...]

(c) that of a person acting for the Scottish Ambulance Service Board in exercise of the function referred to in article 4(1)(a) of the Scottish Ambulance Service Board Order 1999 (S.I. 1999/686) (exercise by the Board of function of providing ambulances and other means of transport for ill and other persons).

[(d) that of a registered medical practitioner;

(e) that of a registered nurse; or

(f) that of a registered midwife]

2 Assaulting or impeding certain emergency workers responding to emergency circumstances

(1) A person who assaults, obstructs or hinders another while that other person is, in a capacity mentioned in subsection (3) below, responding to emergency circumstances, commits an offence.

(2) No offence is committed under subsection (1) above unless the person who assaults, obstructs or hinders knows or ought to know that the person being assaulted, obstructed or hindered—

(a) is acting in that capacity; and

(b) is or might be responding—

(i) to emergency circumstances; or

(ii) as if there were emergency circumstances.

(3) The capacity referred to in subsection (1) above is—

(a) that of a prison officer, that is to say—

(i) a person who holds a post, otherwise than as a medical officer, to which the person has been appointed for the purposes of section 3(1A) of the Prisons (Scotland) Act 1989 (c. 45); or

(ii) a prisoner custody officer within the meaning of Chapter II of Part VIII of the Criminal Justice and Public Order Act 1994 (c. 33);

(b) that of a member of Her Majesty's Coastguard;

(c) that of a member of the crew of a vessel operated by—

(i) the Royal National Lifeboat Institution; or

(ii) any other person or organisation operating a vessel for the purpose of providing a rescue service on a body of water,

or a person who musters the crew of such a vessel or attends to its launch;

(d) [...]

(e) [...]

(f) [...]

(g) that of a social worker, within the meaning given by section 77(1) of the Regulation of Care (Scotland) Act 2001 (asp 8), while taking action required or permitted by—

(i) a child protection order [(as defined in section 202(1) of the Children's Hearings (Scotland) Act 2011 (asp 1)]; or

[(ii) an order under section 55 of that Act of 2011 (emergency order for removal of child),]

(h) that of a mental health officer, that is to say—

(i) a mental health officer within the meaning given by section 32(1) of the Mental Health (Care and Treatment) (Scotland) Act 2003 (asp 13); or

(ii) until section 32(1) of that Act (appointment and deemed appointment of mental health officers) comes into force, a mental health officer within the meaning given by section 125 of the Mental Health (Scotland) Act 1984 (c. 36).

(4) For the purposes of this section and section 3 of this Act, a person is responding to emergency circumstances if the person—

(a) is going anywhere for the purpose of dealing with emergency circumstances occurring there; or

(b) is dealing with emergency circumstances or preparing to do so.

(5) For the purposes of this Act, circumstances are 'emergency' circumstances if they are present or imminent and—

(a) are causing or are likely to cause—

(i) serious injury to or the serious illness (including mental illness) of a person;

(ii) serious harm to the environment (including the life and health of plants and animals and the fabric of buildings); or

(iii) a worsening of any such injury, illness or harm; or

(b) are likely to cause the death of a person.

3 Assaulting or impeding persons assisting emergency workers

(1) A person who assaults, obstructs or hinders another in the circumstances described in subsection (2) below commits an offence.

(2) Those circumstances are where the person being assaulted, obstructed or hindered is assisting another while that other person is, in a capacity mentioned in section 1(3) or 2(3) of this Act, responding to emergency circumstances.

(3) No offence is committed under subsection (1) above unless the person who assaults, obstructs or hinders knows or ought to know—

(a) that the person being assisted is acting in that capacity;

(b) that the person being assisted is or might be responding—

(i) to emergency circumstances; or

(ii) as if there were emergency circumstances; and

(c) that the person being assaulted, obstructed or hindered is assisting the person acting in that capacity.

4 Provisions supplementary to sections 1 to 3

(1) A person may be convicted of the offence under section 1, 2 or 3 of this Act of obstructing or hindering notwithstanding that it is—

(a) effected by means other than physical means; or

(b) effected by action directed only at any vehicle, apparatus, equipment or other thing or any animal used or to be used by a person referred to in that section.

(2) A person who gives false information with the intention that a person acting in a capacity mentioned in subsection (3) of section 1 of this Act will act upon that information is to be regarded, for the purposes of that section, as hindering the person acting in that capacity.

(3) A person who gives false information with the intention that a person acting in a capacity mentioned in subsection (3) of section 2 of this Act will, while responding to emergency circumstances or instead of doing so, act upon that information is to be regarded, for the purposes of that section, as hindering the person acting in that capacity.

(4) Subsections (2) and (3) above do not prejudice the generality of subsection (1)(a) above.

(5) For the purposes of sections 2 and 3 of this Act, circumstances to which a person is responding are to be taken to be emergency circumstances if the person believes and has reasonable grounds for believing they are or may be emergency circumstances.

(6) Evidence from a single source is sufficient evidence to establish, for the purposes of section 1, 2 or 3 of this Act, whether a person is acting in a capacity referred to in that section.

5 Assaulting or impeding health workers in hospital premises

(1) A person who, in a hospital or on land adjacent to and used wholly or mainly for the purposes of a hospital, assaults, obstructs or hinders a person acting in a capacity mentioned in subsection (3) below or a person assisting such a person commits an offence.

(2) No offence is committed under subsection (1) above unless the person who assaults, obstructs or hinders knows or ought to know that the person being assaulted, obstructed or hindered is acting in that capacity or, as the case may be, that the person being assisted is acting in that capacity and that the person being assaulted, obstructed or hindered is assisting the person acting in that capacity.

(3) The capacity referred to in subsection (1) above is—

(a) that of a registered medical practitioner;

(b) that of a registered nurse;

(c) that of a registered midwife; or

(d) that of a person acting for the Scottish Ambulance Service Board in the exercise of the function referred to in article 4(1)(a) of the Scottish Ambulance Service Board Order 1999 (S.I. 1999/686) (exercise by the Board of function of providing ambulances and other means of transport for ill and other persons).

(4) A person may be convicted of the offence under subsection (1) above of obstructing or hindering notwithstanding that it is—

(a) effected by means other than physical means;

(b) effected by action directed only at any vehicle, apparatus, equipment or other thing used or to be used by a person referred to in that subsection.

(5) Evidence from a single source is sufficient to establish, for the purposes of subsection (1) above, whether a person is acting in a capacity referred to in subsection (3) above.

SEXUAL OFFENCES (SCOTLAND) ACT 2009
(2009, asp 9)

PART 1
RAPE ETC.

Rape

1 Rape

(1) If a person ('A'), with A's penis—

(a) without another person ('B') consenting, and

(b) without any reasonable belief that B consents,

penetrates to any extent, either intending to do so or reckless as to whether there is penetration, the vagina, anus or mouth of B then A commits an offence, to be known as the offence of rape.

(2) For the purposes of this section, penetration is a continuing act from entry until withdrawal of the penis; but this subsection is subject to subsection (3).

(3) In a case where penetration is initially consented to but at some point of time the consent is withdrawn, subsection (2) is to be construed as if the reference in it to a continuing act from entry were a reference to a continuing act from that point of time.

(4) In this Act—

'penis' includes a surgically constructed penis if it forms part of A, having been created in the course of surgical treatment, and

'vagina' includes—

(a) the vulva, and

(b) a surgically constructed vagina (together with any surgically constructed vulva), if it forms part of B, having been created in the course of such treatment.

Sexual assault by penetration

2 Sexual assault by penetration

(1) If a person ('A'), with any part of A's body or anything else—

(a) without another person ('B') consenting, and

(b) without any reasonable belief that B consents,

penetrates sexually to any extent, either intending to do so or reckless as to whether there is penetration, the vagina or anus of B then A commits an offence, to be known as the offence of sexual assault by penetration.

(2) For the purposes of this section, penetration is a continuing act from entry to withdrawal of whatever is intruded; but this subsection is subject to subsection (3).

(3) In a case where penetration is initially consented to but at some point of time the consent is withdrawn, subsection (2) is to be construed as if the reference in it to a continuing act from entry were a reference to a continuing act from that point of time.

(4) Without prejudice to the generality of subsection (1), the reference in that subsection to penetration with any part of A's body is to be construed as including a reference to penetration with A's penis.

Sexual assault and other sexual offences

3 Sexual assault

(1) If a person ('A')—

(a) without another person ('B') consenting, and

(b) without any reasonable belief that B consents,

does any of the things mentioned in subsection (2), then A commits an offence, to be known as the offence of sexual assault.

(2) Those things are, that A—

(a) penetrates sexually, by any means and to any extent, either intending to do so or reckless as to whether there is penetration, the vagina, anus or mouth of B,

(b) intentionally or recklessly touches B sexually,

(c) engages in any other form of sexual activity in which A, intentionally or recklessly, has physical contact (whether bodily contact or contact by means of an implement and whether or not through clothing) with B,

(d) intentionally or recklessly ejaculates semen onto B,

(e) intentionally or recklessly emits urine or saliva onto B sexually.

(3) For the purposes of paragraph (a) of subsection (2), penetration is a continuing act from entry until withdrawal of whatever is intruded; but this subsection is subject to subsection (4).

(4) In a case where penetration is initially consented to but at some point of time the consent is withdrawn, subsection (3) is to be construed as if the reference in it to a continuing act from entry were a reference to a continuing act from that point of time.

(5) Without prejudice to the generality of paragraph (a) of subsection (2), the reference in the paragraph to penetration by any means is to be construed as including a reference to penetration with A's penis.

4 Sexual coercion

If a person ('A')—

(a) without another person ('B') consenting to participate in a sexual activity, and

(b) without any reasonable belief that B consents to participating in that activity,

intentionally causes B to participate in that activity, then A commits an offence, to be known as the offence of sexual coercion.

5 Coercing a person into being present during a sexual activity

(1) If a person ('A')—

(a) without another person ('B') consenting, and

(b) without any reasonable belief that B consents,

either intentionally engages in a sexual activity and for a purpose mentioned in subsection (2) does so in the presence of B or intentionally and for a purpose mentioned in that subsection causes B to be present while a third person engages in such an activity, then A commits an offence, to be known as the offence of coercing a person into being present during a sexual activity.

(2) The purposes are—

(a) obtaining sexual gratification,

(b) humiliating, distressing or alarming B.

(3) Without prejudice to the generality of subsection (1), the reference in that subsection—

(a) to A engaging in a sexual activity in the presence of B, includes a reference to A engaging in it in a place in which A can be observed by B other than by B looking at an image, and

(b) to B being present while a third person engages in such an activity, includes a reference to B being in a place from which the third person can be so observed by B.

6 Coercing a person into looking at a sexual image

(1) If a person ('A') intentionally and for a purpose mentioned in subsection (2) causes another person ('B')—

(a) without B consenting, and

(b) without any reasonable belief that B consents,

to look at a sexual image, then A commits an offence, to be known as the offence of coercing a person into looking at a sexual image.

(2) The purposes are—

(a) obtaining sexual gratification,

(b) humiliating, distressing or alarming B.

(3) For the purposes of subsection (1), a sexual image is an image (produced by whatever means and whether or not a moving image) of—

(a) A engaging in a sexual activity or of a third person or imaginary person so engaging,

(b) A's genitals or the genitals of a third person or imaginary person.

7 Communicating indecently etc.

(1) If a person ('A'), intentionally and for a purpose mentioned in subsection (3), sends, by whatever means, a sexual written communication to or directs, by whatever means, a sexual verbal communication at, another person ('B')—

(a) without B consenting to its being so sent or directed, and

(b) without any reasonable belief that B consents to its being so sent or directed,

then A commits an offence, to be known as the offence of communicating indecently.

(2) If, in circumstances other than are as mentioned in subsection (1), a person ('A'), intentionally and for a purpose mentioned in subsection (3), causes another person ('B') to see or hear, by whatever means, a sexual written communication or sexual verbal communication—

(a) without B consenting to seeing or as the case may be hearing it, and

(b) without any reasonable belief that B consents to seeing or as the case may be hearing it,

then A commits an offence, to be known as the offence of causing a person to see or hear an indecent communication.

(3) The purposes are—

(a) obtaining sexual gratification,

(b) humiliating, distressing or alarming B.

(4) In this section—

'written communication' means a communication in whatever written form, and without prejudice to that generality includes a communication which comprises writings of a person other than A (as for example a passage in a book or magazine), and

'verbal communication' means a communication in whatever verbal form, and without prejudice to that generality includes—

(a) a communication which comprises sounds of sexual activity (whether actual or simulated), and

(b) a communication by means of sign language.

8 Sexual exposure

(1) If a person ('A')—

(a) without another person ('B') consenting, and

(b) without any reasonable belief that B consents,

intentionally and for a purpose mentioned in subsection (2), exposes A's genitals in a sexual manner to B with the intention that B will see them, then A commits an offence, to be known as the offence of sexual exposure.

(2) The purposes are—

(a) obtaining sexual gratification,

(b) humiliating, distressing or alarming B.

9 Voyeurism

(1) A person ('A') commits an offence, to be known as the offence of voyeurism, if A does any of the things mentioned in subsections (2) to (5).

(2) The first thing is that A—

(a) without another person ('B') consenting, and

(b) without any reasonable belief that B consents,

for a purpose mentioned in subsection (6) observes B doing a private act.

(3) The second thing is that A—

(a) without another person ('B') consenting, and

(b) without any reasonable belief that B consents,

operates equipment with the intention of enabling A or another person ('C'), for a purpose mentioned in subsection (7), to observe B doing a private act.

(4) The third thing is that A—

(a) without another person ('B') consenting, and

(b) without any reasonable belief that B consents,

records B doing a private act with the intention that A or another person ('C'), for a purpose mentioned in subsection (7), will look at an image of B doing the act.

[(4A) The fourth thing is that A—

(a) without another person ('B') consenting, and

(b) without any reasonable belief that B consents,

operates equipment beneath B's clothing with the intention of enabling A or another person ('C'), for a purpose mentioned in subsection (7), to observe B's genitals or buttocks (whether exposed or covered with underwear) or the underwear covering B's genitals or buttocks, in circumstances where the genitals, buttocks or underwear would not otherwise be visible.

(4B) The fifth thing is that A—

(a) without another person ('B') consenting, and

(b) without any reasonable belief that B consents,

records an image beneath B's clothing of B's genitals or buttocks (whether exposed or covered with underwear) or the underwear covering B's genitals or buttocks, in circumstances where the genitals, buttocks or underwear would not otherwise be visible, with the intention that A or another person ('C'), for a purpose mentioned in subsection (7), will look at the image.]

(5) The [sixth] thing is that A—

(a) installs equipment, or

[(b) constructs or adapts a structure or part of a structure, with the intention of enabling A or another person to do an act referred to in subsection (2), (3), (4), (4A) or (4B).]

(6) The purposes referred to in subsection (2) are—

(a) obtaining sexual gratification,

(b) humiliating, distressing or alarming B.

(7) The purposes referred to in subsections (3) [, (4), (4A) and (4B)] are—

(a) obtaining sexual gratification (whether for A or C),

(b) humiliating, distressing or alarming B.

10 Interpretation of section 9

(1) For the purposes of section 9, a person is doing a private act if the person is in a place which in the circumstances would reasonably be expected to provide privacy, and—

(a) the person's genitals, buttocks or breasts are exposed or covered only with underwear,

(b) the person is using a lavatory, or

(c) the person is doing a sexual act that is not of a kind ordinarily done in public.

(2) For the purposes of section 9(3) [and (4A)], operating equipment includes enabling or securing its activation by another person without that person's knowledge.

(3) In section 9(5), 'structure' includes a tent, vehicle or vessel or other temporary or movable structure.

11 Administering a substance for sexual purposes

(1) If a person ('A') intentionally administers a substance to, or causes a substance to be taken by, another person ('B')—

(a) without B knowing, and

(b) without any reasonable belief that B knows,

and does so for the purpose of stupefying or overpowering B, so as to enable any person to engage in a sexual activity which involves B, then A commits an offence, to be known as the offence of administering a substance for sexual purposes.

(2) For the purposes of subsection (1), if A, whether by act or omission, induces in B a reasonable belief that the substance administered or taken is (either or both)—

(a) of a substantially lesser strength, or

(b) in a substantially lesser quantity,

than it is, any knowledge which B has (or belief as to knowledge which B has) that it is being administered or taken is to be disregarded.

PART 2
CONSENT AND REASONABLE BELIEF

Consent

12 Meaning of 'consent' and related expressions

In Parts 1 and 3, 'consent' means free agreement (and related expressions are to be construed accordingly).

13 Circumstances in which conduct takes place without free agreement

(1) For the purposes of section 12, but without prejudice to the generality of that section, free agreement to conduct is absent in the circumstances set out in subsection (2).

(2) Those circumstances are—

(a) where the conduct occurs at a time when B is incapable because of the effect of alcohol or any other substance of consenting to it,

(b) where B agrees or submits to the conduct because of violence used against B or any other person, or because of threats of violence made against B or any other person,

(c) where B agrees or submits to the conduct because B is unlawfully detained by A,

(d) where B agrees or submits to the conduct because B is mistaken, as a result of deception by A, as to the nature or purpose of the conduct,

(e) where B agrees or submits to the conduct because A induces B to agree or submit to the conduct by impersonating a person known personally to B, or

(f) where the only expression or indication of agreement to the conduct is from a person other than B.

(3) References in this section to A and to B are to be construed in accordance with sections 1 to 9.

14 Consent: capacity while asleep or unconscious

(1) This section applies in relation to sections 1 to 9.

(2) A person is incapable, while asleep or unconscious, of consenting to any conduct.

15 Consent: scope and withdrawal

(1) This section applies in relation to sections 1 to 9.

(2) Consent to conduct does not of itself imply consent to any other conduct.

(3) Consent to conduct may be withdrawn at any time before, or in the case of continuing conduct, during, the conduct.

(4) If the conduct takes place, or continues to take place, after consent has been withdrawn, it takes place, or continues to take place, without consent.

Reasonable belief

16 Reasonable belief

In determining, for the purposes of Part 1, whether a person's belief as to consent or knowledge was reasonable, regard is to be had to whether the person took any steps to ascertain whether there was consent or, as the case may be, knowledge; and if so, to what those steps were.

PART 3
MENTALLY DISORDERED PERSONS

Mentally disordered persons

17 Capacity to consent

(1) This section applies in relation to sections 1 to 9.

(2) A mentally disordered person is incapable of consenting to conduct where, by reason of mental disorder, the person is unable to do one or more of the following—

(a) understand what the conduct is,

(b) form a decision as to whether to engage in the conduct (or as to whether the conduct should take place),

(c) communicate any such decision.

(3) In this Act, 'mental disorder' has the same meaning as in section 328 of the Mental Health (Care and Treatment) (Scotland) Act 2003 (asp 13) (and related expressions are to be construed accordingly).

PART 4
CHILDREN

Young children

18 Rape of a young child

If a person ('A'), with A's penis, penetrates to any extent, either intending to do so or reckless as to whether there is penetration, the vagina, anus or mouth of a child ('B') who has not attained the age of 13 years, then A commits an offence, to be known as the offence of rape of a young child.

19 Sexual assault on a young child by penetration

(1) If a person ('A'), with any part of A's body or anything else, penetrates sexually to any extent, either intending to do so or reckless as to whether there is penetration, the vagina or anus of a child ('B') who has not attained the age of 13

years, then A commits an offence, to be known as the offence of sexual assault on a young child by penetration.

(2) Without prejudice to the generality of subsection (1), the reference in that subsection to penetration with any part of A's body is to be construed as including a reference to penetration with A's penis.

20 Sexual assault on a young child

(1) If a person ('A') does any of the things mentioned in subsection (2) ('B' being in each case a child who has not attained the age of 13 years), then A commits an offence, to be known as the offence of sexual assault on a young child.

(2) Those things are, that A—

(a) penetrates sexually, by any means and to any extent, either intending to do so or reckless as to whether there is penetration, the vagina, anus or mouth of B,

(b) intentionally or recklessly touches B sexually,

(c) engages in any other form of sexual activity in which A, intentionally or recklessly, has physical contact (whether bodily contact or contact by means of an implement and whether or not through clothing) with B,

(d) intentionally or recklessly ejaculates semen onto B,

(e) intentionally or recklessly emits urine or saliva onto B sexually.

(3) Without prejudice to the generality of paragraph (a) of subsection (2), the reference in the paragraph to penetration by any means is to be construed as including a reference to penetration with A's penis.

21 Causing a young child to participate in a sexual activity

If a person ('A') intentionally causes a child ('B') who has not attained the age of 13 years to participate in a sexual activity, then A commits an offence, to be known as the offence of causing a young child to participate in a sexual activity.

22 Causing a young child to be present during a sexual activity

(1) If a person ('A') either—

(a) intentionally engages in a sexual activity and for a purpose mentioned in subsection (2) does so in the presence of a child ('B') who has not attained the age of 13 years, or

(b) intentionally and for a purpose mentioned in subsection (2) causes B to be present while a third person engages in such an activity,

then A commits an offence, to be known as the offence of causing a young child to be present during a sexual activity.

(2) The purposes are—

(a) obtaining sexual gratification,

(b) humiliating, distressing or alarming B.

(3) Without prejudice to the generality of subsection (1), the reference—

(a) in paragraph (a) of that subsection to A engaging in a sexual activity in the presence of B, includes a reference to A engaging in it in a place in which A can be observed by B other than by B looking at an image, and

(b) in paragraph (b) of that subsection to B being present while a third person engages in such an activity, includes a reference to B being in a place from which the third person can be so observed by B.

23 Causing a young child to look at a sexual image

(1) If a person ('A') intentionally and for a purpose mentioned in subsection (2) causes a child ('B') who has not attained the age of 13 years to look at a sexual image, then A commits an offence, to be known as the offence of causing a young child to look at a sexual image.

(2) The purposes are—

(a) obtaining sexual gratification,

(b) humiliating, distressing or alarming B.

(3) For the purposes of subsection (1), a sexual image is an image (produced by whatever means and whether or not a moving image) of—

(a) A engaging in a sexual activity or of a third person or imaginary person so engaging,

(b) A's genitals or the genitals of a third person or imaginary person.

24 Communicating indecently with a young child etc.

(1) If a person ('A'), intentionally and for a purpose mentioned in subsection (3)—

(a) sends, by whatever means, a sexual written communication to, or

(b) directs, by whatever means, a sexual verbal communication at,

a child ('B') who has not attained the age of 13 years, then A commits an offence, to be known as the offence of communicating indecently with a young child.

(2) If, in circumstances other than are as mentioned in subsection (1), a person ('A'), intentionally and for a purpose mentioned in subsection (3) causes a child ('B') who has not attained the age of 13 years to see or hear, by whatever means, a sexual written communication or sexual verbal communication, then A commits an offence, to be known as the offence of causing a young child to see or hear an indecent communication.

(3) The purposes are—

(a) obtaining sexual gratification,

(b) humiliating, distressing or alarming B.

(4) In this section—

'written communication' means a communication in whatever written form, and without prejudice to that generality includes a communication which comprises writings of a person other than A (as for example a passage in a book or magazine), and

'verbal communication' means a communication in whatever verbal form, and without prejudice to that generality includes—

(a) a communication which comprises sounds of sexual activity (whether actual or simulated), and

(b) a communication by means of sign language.

25 Sexual exposure to a young child

(1) If a person ('A') intentionally and for a purpose mentioned in subsection (2) exposes A's genitals in a sexual manner to a child ('B') who has not attained the age of 13 years, with the intention that B will see them, then A commits an offence, to be known as the offence of sexual exposure to a young child.

(2) The purposes are—

(a) obtaining sexual gratification,

(b) humiliating, distressing or alarming B.

26 Voyeurism towards a young child

(1) If a person ('A') does any of the things mentioned in subsections (2) to (5) in relation to a child ('B') who has not attained the age of 13 years, then A commits an offence, to be known as the offence of voyeurism towards a young child.

(2) The first thing is that A, for a purpose mentioned in subsection (6), observes B doing a private act.

(3) The second thing is that A operates equipment with the intention of enabling A or another person ('C'), for a purpose mentioned in subsection (7), to observe B doing a private act.

(4) The third thing is that A records B doing a private act with the intention that A or another person ('C'), for a purpose mentioned in subsection (7), will look at an image of B doing the act.

[(4A) The fourth thing is that A operates equipment beneath B's clothing with the intention of enabling A or another person ('C'), for a purpose mentioned in subsection (7), to observe—

(a) B's genitals or buttocks (whether exposed or covered with underwear), or

(b) the underwear covering B's genitals or buttocks,

in circumstances where the genitals, buttocks or underwear would not otherwise be visible.

(4B) The fifth thing is that A records an image beneath B's clothing of—

(a) B's genitals or buttocks (whether exposed or covered with underwear), or

(b) the underwear covering B's genitals or buttocks,

in circumstances where the genitals, buttocks or underwear would not otherwise be visible, with the intention that A or another person ('C'), for a purpose mentioned in subsection (7), will look at the image.]

(5) The [sixth] thing is that A—

(a) installs equipment, or

[(b) constructs or adapts a structure or part of a structure, with the intention of enabling A or another person to do an act referred to in subsection (2), (3), (4), (4A) or (4B).]

(6) The purposes referred to in subsection (2) are—

(a) obtaining sexual gratification,

(b) humiliating, distressing or alarming B.

(7) The purposes referred to in subsections (3) [, (4), (4A) and (4B)] are—

(a) obtaining sexual gratification (whether for A or C),

(b) humiliating, distressing or alarming B.

(8) Section 10 applies for the purposes of this section as it applies for the purposes of section 9 (the references in that section to section 9(3) [, (4A)] and (5) being construed as references to subsections (3) [, (4A)] and (5) of this section).

27 Belief that child had attained the age of 13 years

It is not a defence to a charge in proceedings under any of sections 18 to 26 that A believed that B had attained the age of 13 years.

Older children

28 Having intercourse with an older child

If a person ('A'), who has attained the age of 16 years, with A's penis, penetrates to any extent, either intending to do so or reckless as to whether there is penetration, the vagina, anus or mouth of a child ('B'), who—

(a) has attained the age of 13 years, but

(b) has not attained the age of 16 years,

then A commits an offence, to be known as the offence of having intercourse with an older child.

29 Engaging in penetrative sexual activity with or towards an older child

(1) If a person ('A'), who has attained the age of 16 years, with any part of A's body or anything else penetrates sexually to any extent, either intending to do so or reckless as to whether there is penetration, the vagina or anus of a child ('B') who—

(a) has attained the age of 13 years, but

(b) has not attained the age of 16 years,

then A commits an offence, to be known as the offence of engaging in penetrative sexual activity with or towards an older child.

(2) Without prejudice to the generality of subsection (1), the reference in that paragraph to penetration with any part of A's body is to be construed as including a reference to penetration with A's penis.

30 Engaging in sexual activity with or towards an older child

(1) If a person ('A'), who has attained the age of 16 years, does any of the things mentioned in subsection (2) 'B' being in each case a child who—

(a) has attained the age of 13 years, but

(b) has not attained the age of 16 years,

then A commits an offence, to be known as the offence of engaging in sexual activity with or towards an older child.

(2) Those things are, that A—

(a) penetrates sexually, by any means and to any extent, either intending to do so or reckless as to whether there is penetration, the vagina, anus or mouth of B,

(b) intentionally or recklessly touches B sexually,

(c) engages in any other form of sexual activity in which A, intentionally or recklessly, has physical contact (whether bodily contact or contact by means of an implement and whether or not through clothing) with B,

(d) intentionally or recklessly ejaculates semen onto B,

(e) intentionally or recklessly emits urine or saliva onto B sexually.

(3) Without prejudice to the generality of paragraph (a) of subsection (2), the reference in the paragraph to penetration by any means is to be construed as including a reference to penetration with A's penis.

31 Causing an older child to participate in a sexual activity

If a person ('A'), who has attained the age of 16 years, intentionally causes a child ('B'), who—

(a) has attained the age of 13 years, but

(b) has not attained the age of 16 years,

to participate in a sexual activity, then A commits an offence, to be known as the offence of causing an older child to participate in a sexual activity.

32 Causing an older child to be present during a sexual activity

(1) If a person ('A'), who has attained the age of 16 years either—

(a) intentionally engages in a sexual activity and for a purpose mentioned in subsection (2) does so in the presence of a child ('B'), who—

(i) has attained the age of 13 years, but

(ii) has not attained the age of 16 years, or

(b) intentionally, and for a purpose mentioned in subsection (2) causes B to be present while a third person engages in such an activity,

then A commits an offence, to be known as the offence of causing an older child to be present during a sexual activity.

(2) The purposes are—

(a) obtaining sexual gratification,

(b) humiliating, distressing or alarming B.

(3) Without prejudice to the generality of subsection (1), the reference—

(a) in paragraph (a) of that subsection to A engaging in a sexual activity in the presence of B, includes a reference to

A engaging in it in a place in which A can be observed by B other than by B looking at an image, and

(b) in paragraph (b) of that subsection to B being present while a third person engages in such an activity, includes a reference to B being in a place from which the third person can be so observed by B.

33 Causing an older child to look at a sexual image

(1) If a person ('A'), who has attained the age of 16 years, intentionally and for a purpose mentioned in subsection (2) causes a child ('B'), who—

(a) has attained the age of 13 years, but

(b) has not attained the age of 16 years,

to look at a sexual image, then A commits an offence, to be known as the offence of causing an older child to look at a sexual image.

(2) The purposes are—

(a) obtaining sexual gratification,

(b) humiliating, distressing or alarming B.

(3) For the purposes of subsection (1), a sexual image is an image (produced by whatever means and whether or not a moving image) of—

(a) A engaging in a sexual activity or of a third person or imaginary person so engaging,

(b) A's genitals or the genitals of a third person or imaginary person.

34 Communicating indecently with an older child etc.

(1) If a person ('A'), who has attained the age of 16 years, intentionally and for a purpose mentioned in subsection (3), sends, by whatever means, a sexual written communication to or directs, by whatever means, a sexual verbal communication at, a child ('B') who—

(a) has attained the age of 13 years, but

(b) has not attained the age of 16 years,

then A commits an offence, to be known as the offence of communicating indecently with an older child.

(2) If, in circumstances other than are as mentioned in subsection (1), a person ('A'), who has attained the age of 16 years, intentionally and for a purpose mentioned in subsection (3), causes another person ('B') who is a child described in paragraphs (a) and (b) of subsection (1) to see or hear, by whatever means, a sexual written communication or sexual verbal communication, then A commits an offence, to be known as the offence of causing an older child to see or hear an indecent communication.

(3) The purposes are—

(a) obtaining sexual gratification,

(b) humiliating, distressing or alarming B.

(4) In this section—

'written communication' means a communication in whatever written form, and without prejudice to that generality includes a communication which comprises writings of a person other than A (as for example a passage in a book or magazine), and

'verbal communication' means a communication in whatever verbal form, and without prejudice to that generality includes—

(a) a communication which comprises sounds of sexual activity (whether actual or simulated), and

(b) a communication by means of sign language.

35 Sexual exposure to an older child

(1) If a person ('A'), who has attained the age of 16 years, intentionally and for a purpose mentioned in subsection (2) exposes A's genitals in a sexual manner to a child ('B') who—

(a) has attained the age of 13 years, but

(b) has not attained the age of 16 years,

with the intention that B will see them, then A commits an offence, to be known as the offence of sexual exposure to an older child.

(2) The purposes are—

(a) obtaining sexual gratification,

(b) humiliating, distressing or alarming B.

36 Voyeurism towards an older child

(1) If a person ('A'), who has attained the age of 16 years, does any of the things mentioned in subsections (2) to (5) in relation to a child ('B') who—

(a) has attained the age of 13 years, but

(b) has not attained the age of 16 years,

then A commits an offence, to be known as the offence of voyeurism towards an older child.

(2) The first thing is that A, for a purpose mentioned in subsection (6), observes B doing a private act.

(3) The second thing is that A operates equipment with the intention of enabling A or another person ('C'), for a purpose mentioned in subsection (7), to observe B doing a private act.

(4) The third thing is that A records B doing a private act with the intention that A or another person ('C'), for a purpose mentioned in subsection (7), will look at an image of B doing the act.

[(4A) The fourth thing is that A operates equipment beneath B's clothing with the intention of enabling A or another person ('C'), for a purpose mentioned in subsection (7), to observe—

(a) B's genitals or buttocks (whether exposed or covered with underwear), or

(b) the underwear covering B's genitals or buttocks,

in circumstances where the genitals, buttocks or underwear would not otherwise be visible.

(4B) The fifth thing is that A records an image beneath B's clothing of—

(a) B's genitals or buttocks (whether exposed or covered with underwear), or

(b) the underwear covering B's genitals or buttocks,

in circumstances where the genitals, buttocks or underwear would not otherwise be visible, with the intention that A or another person ('C'), for a purpose mentioned in subsection (7), will look at the image.]

(5) The [sixth] thing is that A—

(a) installs equipment, or

[(b) constructs or adapts a structure or part of a structure, with the intention of enabling A or another person to do an act referred to in subsection (2), (3), (4), (4A) or (4B).]

(6) The purposes referred to in subsection (2) are—

(a) obtaining sexual gratification,

(b) humiliating, distressing or alarming B.

(7) The purposes referred to in subsections (3) [, (4), (4A) and (4B)] are—

(a) obtaining sexual gratification (whether for A or C),

(b) humiliating, distressing or alarming B.

(8) Section 10 applies for the purposes of this section as it applies for the purposes of section 9 (the references in that section to section 9(3) [, (4A)] and (5) being construed as references to subsections (3) [, (4A)] and (5) of this section).

37 Older children engaging in sexual conduct with each other

(1) If a child ('A'), being a child mentioned in subsection (2), does any of the things mentioned in subsection (3), 'B' being in each case a child mentioned in subsection (2), then A commits an offence, to be known as the offence of engaging while an older child in sexual conduct with or towards another older child.

(2) The child is a child who—

(a) has attained the age of 13 years, but

(b) has not attained the age of 16 years.

(3) The things are that A—

(a) penetrates sexually, with A's penis and to any extent, either intending to do so or reckless as to whether there is penetration, the vagina, anus or mouth of B,

(b) intentionally or recklessly touches the vagina, anus or penis of B sexually with A's mouth.

(4) In the circumstances specified in subsection (1), if B engages by consent in the conduct in question, then B commits an offence, to be known as the offence of engaging while an older child in consensual sexual conduct with another older child.

(5) In paragraph (b) of subsection (3), the reference to A's mouth is to be construed as including a reference to A's tongue or teeth.

38 Penetration and consent for the purposes of section 37

(1) This section applies for the purposes of section 37.

(2) Penetration is a continuing act from entry until withdrawal of whatever is intruded.

(3) 'Consent' means free agreement (and related expressions are to be construed accordingly).

(4) Without prejudice to the generality of subsection (3), free agreement to conduct is absent in the circumstances set out in section 13(2) (references in that section to A and B being construed in accordance with section 37).

(5) A person is incapable, while asleep or unconscious, of consenting to any conduct.

(6) Consent to conduct does not of itself imply consent to any other conduct.

(7) Consent to conduct may be withdrawn at any time before, or in the case of continuing conduct, during, the conduct.

(8) If the conduct takes place, or continues to take place, after consent has been withdrawn, it takes place, or continues to take place, without consent.

39 Defences in relation to offences against older children

(1) It is a defence to a charge in proceedings—

(a) against A under any of sections 28 to 37(1) that A reasonably believed that B had attained the age of 16 years,

(b) against B under section 37(4) that B reasonably believed that A had attained the age of 16 years.

(2) But—

(a) the defence under subsection (1)(a) is not available to A—

(i) if A has previously been charged by the police with a relevant sexual offence, [...]

[(ia) if A has a previous conviction for a relevant foreign offence committed against a person under the age of 16 [and the court before which the charge is brought considers it is appropriate for that conviction to have that effect], or]

(ii) if there is in force in respect of A a risk of sexual harm order,

(b) the defence under subsection (1)(b) is not available to B—

(i) if B has previously been charged by the police with a relevant sexual offence, [...]

[(ia) if B has a previous conviction for a relevant foreign offence committed against a person under the age of 16 [and the court before which the charge is brought considers it is appropriate for that conviction to have that effect], or]

(ii) if there is in force in respect of B a risk of sexual harm order.

(3) It is a defence to a charge in proceedings under any of the sections mentioned in subsection (4) that at the time when the conduct to which the charge relates took place, the difference between A's age and B's age did not exceed 2 years.

(4) Those sections are—

(a) section 30(2)(a), but not in so far as the charge is founded on—

(i) penetration of B's vagina, anus or mouth with A's penis,

(ii) penetration of B's vagina or anus with A's mouth, tongue or teeth,

(b) section 30(2)(b) or (c), but not in so far as the charge is founded on sexual touching or other physical activity involving—

(i) B's vagina, anus or penis being touched sexually by A's mouth,

(ii) A's vagina, anus or mouth being penetrated by B's penis,

(iii) A's vagina, anus or penis being touched sexually by B's mouth,

(c) section 30(2)(d) [or (e)],

(d) any of sections 31 to 36.

(5) In paragraphs (a) and (b) of subsection (2)—

(a) 'a relevant sexual offence' means an offence listed in schedule 1,

[(aa) 'a previous conviction for a relevant foreign offence' means a previous conviction by a court in a member State of the European Union [...] for an offence that is equivalent to one listed in paragraph 1, 4, 7, 10, 13 (so far as applying to an offence listed in paragraph 1, 4, 7 or 10) or 14 of schedule 1,]

(b) 'a risk of sexual harm order' means an order under section 2 of the Protection of Children and Prevention of Sexual Offences (Scotland) Act 2005 (asp 9) or section 123 of the Sexual Offences Act 2003 (c. 42).

[(5A) Any issue of equivalence arising in pursuance of subsection (5)(aa) is for the court to determine.

(5B) For that purpose, an offence may be equivalent to one listed in paragraph 1, 4, 7, 10, 13 (so far as applying to an offence listed in paragraph 1, 4, 7 or 10) or 14 of schedule 1 even though, under the law of the member State (or part of the member State) in question, it is an offence—

(a) regardless of the age of the victim, or

(b) only if committed against a person under an age other than 16 years.]

(6) The Scottish Ministers may by order modify schedule 1 so as to add an offence against a child which involves sexual conduct or delete an offence listed there.

(7) It is not a defence to a charge in—

(a) proceedings under any of sections 28 to 37(1) against A that A believed that B had not attained the age of 13 years,

(b) proceedings under section 37(4) against B that B believed that A had not attained the age of 13 years.

General

40 Special provision as regards failure to establish whether child has or has not attained certain ages

(1) Deeming provision 1 applies to a trial where—

(a) A is charged with an offence under any of sections 28 to 36 or 37(1),

(b) there is a failure to establish beyond reasonable doubt that B was a child who had attained the age of 13 years at the relevant time, and

(c) the court or, in the case of a trial of an indictment, the jury is satisfied it is established beyond reasonable doubt that B had not attained the age of 16 years at the time.

(2) Deeming provision 2 applies to a trial where—

(a) B is charged with an offence under section 37(4),

(b) there is a failure to establish beyond reasonable doubt that A was a child who had attained the age of 13 years at the relevant time, and

(c) the court or, in the case of a trial of an indictment, the jury is satisfied it is established beyond reasonable doubt that A had not attained the age of 16 years at the time.

(3) Deeming provision 3 applies to a trial where—

(a) A is charged with an offence under section 37(1),

(b) there is a failure to establish beyond reasonable doubt that A was a child who had not attained the age of 16 years at the relevant time, and

(c) the court or, in the case of a trial of an indictment, the jury is satisfied it is established beyond reasonable doubt that A had attained the age of 13 years at the time.

(4) Deeming provision 4 applies to a trial where—

(a) B is charged with an offence under section 37(4),

(b) there is a failure to establish beyond reasonable doubt that B was a child who had not attained the age of 16 years at the relevant time, and

(c) the court or, in the case of a trial of an indictment, the jury is satisfied it is established beyond reasonable doubt that B had attained the age of 13 years at the time.

(5) Where any of the deeming provisions apply, references in sections 28 to 37 to A or B having or not having attained a particular age are to be construed in accordance with this section and section 41.

(6) In this section and section 41, the 'relevant time' is when the conduct to which the proceedings relate occurred.

41 Special provision as regards age: deeming provisions
The deeming provisions are—

Deeming provision 1	B is to be deemed for the purposes of the proceedings to be a person who has attained the age of 13 years at the relevant time.
Deeming provision 2	A is to be deemed for the purposes of the proceedings to be a person who has attained the age of 13 years at the relevant time.
Deeming provision 3	A is to be deemed for the purposes of the proceedings to be a child who has not attained the age of 16 years at the relevant time.
Deeming provision 4	B is to be deemed for the purposes of the proceedings to be a person who has not attained the age of 16 years at the relevant time.

PART 5
ABUSE OF POSITION OF TRUST

Children

42 Sexual abuse of trust
If a person ('A') who has attained the age of 18 years—
(a) intentionally engages in a sexual activity with or directed towards another person ('B') who is under 18, and
(b) is in a position of trust in relation to B,
then A commits an offence, to be known as the offence of sexual abuse of trust.

43 Positions of trust
(1) For the purposes of section 42, a person ('A') is in a position of trust in relation to another person ('B') if any of the five conditions set out below is fulfilled.

(2) The first condition is that B is detained by virtue of an order of court or under an enactment in an institution and A looks after persons under 18 in that institution.

(3) The second condition is that B is resident in a home or other place in which accommodation is provided by a local authority under section 26(1) of the Children (Scotland) Act 1995 (c. 36) and A looks after persons under 18 in that place.

(4) The third condition is that B is accommodated and cared for in—

(a) a hospital,

(b) accommodation provided by an independent health care service,

(c) accommodation provided by a care home service,

(d) a residential establishment, or

(e) accommodation provided by a school care accommodation service or a secure accommodation service,

and A looks after persons under 18 in that place.

(5) The fourth condition is that B is receiving education at—

(a) a school and A looks after persons under 18 in that school, or

(b) a further or higher education institution and A looks after B in that institution.

(6) The fifth condition is that A—

(a) has any parental responsibilities or parental rights in respect of B,

(b) fulfils any such responsibilities or exercises any such rights under arrangement with a person who has such responsibilities or rights,

(c) had any such responsibilities or rights but no longer has such responsibilities or rights, or

(d) treats B as a child of A's family,

and B is a member of the same household as A.

(7) A looks after a person for the purposes of this section if A regularly cares for, teaches, trains, supervises, or is in sole charge of the person.

(8) The Scottish Ministers may by order modify this section (other than this subsection) and section 44 so as to add, delete or amend a condition.

44 Interpretation of section 43

In section 43—

'care home service' has the meaning given by [paragraph 2 of schedule 12 to the Public Services Reform (Scotland) Act 2010 (asp 8) ('the 2010 Act')],

'further or higher education institution' means a body listed in schedule 2 to the Further and Higher Education (Scotland) Act 2005 (asp 6) [or a college of further education which is assigned to a regional strategic body by order made under section 7C(1) of that Act],

'hospital' means a health service hospital (as defined in section 108(1) of the National Health Service (Scotland) Act 1978 (c. 29)),

['independent health care service' means any of the following—

(a) an independent hospital;

(b) a private psychiatric hospital;

(c) an independent clinic; or

(d) an independent medical agency,

as each of those terms is defined in section 10F(2) of the National Health Service (Scotland) Act 1978 (c.29) ,.]

'local authority' means a council constituted under section 2 of the Local Government etc. (Scotland) Act 1994 (c. 39),

'parental responsibilities' and 'parental rights' have the same meanings as in the Children (Scotland) Act 1995 (c. 36),

'residential establishment' has the meaning given by section 93(1)(a) of that Act of 1995,

'school' has the same meaning as in the Education (Scotland) Act 1980 (c. 44),

'school care accommodation service' has the meaning given by [paragraph 3 of schedule 12 to the 2010 Act], and 'secure accommodation service' has the meaning given by [paragraph 6 of schedule 12 to the 2010 Act].

45 Sexual abuse of trust: defences

(1) It is a defence to a charge in proceedings under section 42 that A reasonably believed—

(a) that B had attained the age of 18, or

(b) that B was not a person in relation to whom A was in a position of trust.

(2) It is a defence to a charge in proceedings under section 42—

(a) that B was A's spouse or civil partner, or

(b) that immediately before the position of trust came into being, a sexual relationship existed between A and B.

(3) Subsection (2) does not apply if A was in a position of trust in relation to B by virtue of section 43(6).

Mentally disordered persons

46 Sexual abuse of trust of a mentally disordered person

(1) If a person ('A')—

(a) intentionally engages in a sexual activity with or directed towards a mentally disordered person ('B'), and

(b) is a person mentioned in subsection (2),

then A commits an offence, to be known as sexual abuse of trust of a mentally disordered person.

(2) Those persons are—

(a) a person providing care services to B,

(b) a person who—

(i) is an individual employed in, or contracted to provide services in or to, or

(ii) not being the Scottish Ministers, is a manager of,

a hospital, independent health care service or state hospital in which B is being given medical treatment.

(3) References in this section to the provision of care services are references to anything done by way of such services—

(a) by,
(b) by an employee of, or
(c) in the course of a service provided or supplied by,

a care service, whether by virtue of a contract of employment or any other contract or in such other circumstances as may be specified in an order made by the Scottish Ministers.

(4) In this section—

['care service' has the meaning given by subsection (1) (a), (b), (d), (f), (g), (j) and (m) of section 47 of the Public Services Reform (Scotland) Act 2010 (asp 8) as read with paragraphs 1, 2, 4, 6, 7, 11 and 19 of schedule 12 to that Act,]

'hospital' and 'independent health care service' have the meanings given in section 44, and

'state hospital' means a hospital provided under section 102(1) of the National Health Service (Scotland) Act 1978 (c. 29).

47 Sexual abuse of trust of a mentally disordered person: defences

(1) It is a defence to a charge in proceedings under section 46 that A reasonably believed—
(a) that B did not have a mental disorder, or
(b) that A was not a person specified in section 46(2).

(2) It is a defence to a charge in proceedings under section 46—
(a) that B was A's spouse or civil partner, or
(b) in a case where A was—
(i) a person specified in section 46(2)(a), that immediately before A began to provide care services to B, a sexual relationship existed between A and B,
(ii) a person specified in section 46(2)(b), that immediately before B was admitted to the hospital (or other establishment) referred to in that provision or (where B has been admitted to that establishment more than once) was last admitted to it, such a relationship existed.

60 Interpretation

(1) In this Act—

'mental disorder' has the meaning given by section 17(3),

'penis' and 'vagina' have the meanings given by section 1(4).

(2) For the purposes of this Act—

(a) penetration, touching, or any other activity,

(b) a communication,

(c) a manner of exposure, or

(d) a relationship,

is sexual if a reasonable person would, in all the circumstances of the case, consider it to be sexual.

CRIMINAL JUSTICE AND LICENSING (SCOTLAND) ACT 2010 (2010, asp 13)

PART 2 CRIMINAL LAW

Serious organised crime

28 Involvement in serious organised crime

(1) A person who agrees with at least one other person to become involved in serious organised crime commits an offence.

(2) Without limiting the generality of subsection (1), a person agrees to become involved in serious organised crime if the person—

(a) agrees to do something (whether or not the doing of that thing would itself constitute an offence), and

(b) knows or suspects, or ought reasonably to have known or suspected, that the doing of that thing will enable or further the commission of serious organised crime.

(3) For the purposes of this section and sections 29 to 31—

'serious organised crime' means crime involving two or more persons acting together for the principal purpose of committing or conspiring to commit a serious offence or a series of serious offences,

'serious offence' means an indictable offence—

(a) committed with the intention of obtaining a material benefit for any person, or

(b) which is an act of violence committed or a threat made with the intention of obtaining such a benefit in the future, and

'material benefit' means a right or interest of any description in any property, whether heritable or moveable and whether corporeal or incorporeal.

(4) A person guilty of an offence under subsection (1) is liable—

(a) on conviction on indictment, to imprisonment for a term not exceeding 10 years or to a fine or to both,

(b) on summary conviction, to imprisonment for a term not exceeding 12 months or to a fine not exceeding the statutory maximum or to both.

29 Offences aggravated by connection with serious organised crime

(1) This subsection applies where it is—

(a) libelled in an indictment or specified in a complaint that an offence is aggravated by a connection with serious organised crime, and

(b) proved that the offence is so aggravated.

(2) An offence is aggravated by a connection with serious organised crime if the person committing the offence is motivated (wholly or partly) by the objective of committing or conspiring to commit serious organised crime.

(3) It is immaterial whether or not in committing the offence the person in fact enables the person or another person to commit serious organised crime.

(4) Evidence from a single source is sufficient to prove that an offence is aggravated by a connection with serious organised crime.

(5) Where subsection (1) applies, the court must—

(a) state on conviction that the offence is aggravated by a connection with serious organised crime,

(b) record the conviction in a way that shows that the offence was so aggravated,

(c) take the aggravation into account in determining the appropriate sentence, and

(d) state—

(i) where the sentence in respect of the offence is different from that which the court would have imposed if the offence were not so aggravated, the extent of and the reasons for that difference, or

(ii) otherwise, the reasons for there being no such difference.

30 Directing serious organised crime

(1) A person commits an offence by directing another person—

(a) to commit a serious offence,

(b) to commit an offence aggravated by a connection with serious organised crime under section 29.

(2) A person commits an offence by directing another person to direct a further person to commit an offence mentioned in subsection (1).

(3) For the purposes of subsections (1) and (2), a person directs another person to commit an offence if the person—

(a) does something, or a series of things, to direct the person to commit the offence,

(b) intends that the thing or things done will persuade the person to commit the offence, and

(c) intends that the thing or things done will—

(i) result in a person committing serious organised crime, or

(ii) enable a person to commit serious organised crime.

(4) The person directing the other person commits an offence under subsection (1) whether or not the other person in fact commits—

(a) a serious offence, or

(b) an offence aggravated by a connection with serious organised crime under section 29.

(5) In this section 'directing' a person to commit an offence includes inciting the person to commit the offence.

(6) A person guilty of an offence under subsection (1) or (2) is liable—

(a) on conviction on indictment, to imprisonment for a term not exceeding 14 years or to a fine or to both,

(b) on summary conviction, to imprisonment for a term not exceeding 12 months or to a fine not exceeding the statutory maximum or to both.

31 Failure to report serious organised crime

(1) This section applies where—

(a) a person ('the person') knows or suspects that another person ('the other person') has committed—

(i) an offence under section 28 or 30, or

(ii) an offence which is aggravated by a connection with serious organised crime under section 29, and

(b) that knowledge or suspicion originates from information obtained—

(i) in the course of the person's trade, profession, business or employment, or

(ii) as a result of a close personal relationship between the person and the other person.

(2) In the case of knowledge or suspicion originating from information obtained by the person as a result of a close personal relationship between the person and the other person, this section applies only where the person has obtained a material benefit as a result of the commission of serious organised crime by the other person.

(3) The person commits an offence if the person does not disclose to a constable—

(a) the person's knowledge or suspicion, and

(b) the information on which that knowledge or suspicion is based.

(4) It is a defence for a person charged with an offence under subsection (3) to prove that the person had a reasonable excuse for not making the disclosure.

(5) Subsection (3) does not require disclosure by a person who is a professional legal adviser (an 'adviser') of—

(a) information which the adviser obtains in privileged circumstances, or

(b) knowledge or a suspicion based on information obtained in privileged circumstances.

(6) For the purpose of subsection (5), information is obtained by an adviser in privileged circumstances if it comes to the adviser, otherwise than for the purposes of committing serious organised crime—

(a) from a client (or from a client's representative) in connection with the provision of legal advice by the adviser to that person,

(b) from a person seeking legal advice from the adviser (or from that person's representative), or

(c) from a person, for the purpose of actual or contemplated legal proceedings.

(7) [...]

(8) A person guilty of an offence under this section is liable—

(a) on conviction on indictment, to imprisonment for a term not exceeding five years or to a fine or to both,

(b) on summary conviction, to imprisonment for a term not exceeding 12 months or to a fine not exceeding the statutory maximum or to both.

Threatening or abusive behaviour

38 Threatening or abusive behaviour

(1) A person ('A') commits an offence if—

(a) A behaves in a threatening or abusive manner,

(b) the behaviour would be likely to cause a reasonable person to suffer fear or alarm, and

(c) A intends by the behaviour to cause fear or alarm or is reckless as to whether the behaviour would cause fear or alarm.

(2) It is a defence for a person charged with an offence under subsection (1) to show that the behaviour was, in the particular circumstances, reasonable.

(3) Subsection (1) applies to—

(a) behaviour of any kind including, in particular, things said or otherwise communicated as well as things done, and

(b) behaviour consisting of—

(i) a single act, or

(ii) a course of conduct.

(4) A person guilty of an offence under subsection (1) is liable—

(a) on conviction on indictment, to imprisonment for a term not exceeding 5 years, or to a fine, or to both, or

(b) on summary conviction, to imprisonment for a term not exceeding 12 months, or to a fine not exceeding the statutory maximum, or to both.

Stalking

39 Offence of stalking

(1) A person ('A') commits an offence, to be known as the offence of stalking, where A stalks another person ('B').

(2) For the purposes of subsection (1), A stalks B where—

(a) A engages in a course of conduct,

(b) subsection (3) or (4) applies, and

(c) A's course of conduct causes B to suffer fear or alarm.

(3) This subsection applies where A engages in the course of conduct with the intention of causing B to suffer fear or alarm.

(4) This subsection applies where A knows, or ought in all the circumstances to have known, that engaging in the course of conduct would be likely to cause B to suffer fear or alarm.

(5) It is a defence for a person charged with an offence under this section to show that the course of conduct—

(a) was authorised by virtue of any enactment or rule of law,

(b) was engaged in for the purpose of preventing or detecting crime, or

(c) was, in the particular circumstances, reasonable.

(6) In this section—

'conduct' means—

(a) following B or any other person,

(b) contacting, or attempting to contact, B or any other person by any means,

(c) publishing any statement or other material—

(i) relating or purporting to relate to B or to any other person,

(ii) purporting to originate from B or from any other person,

(d) monitoring the use by B or by any other person of the internet, email or any other form of electronic communication,

(e) entering any premises,

(f) loitering in any place (whether public or private),

(g) interfering with any property in the possession of B or of any other person,

(h) giving anything to B or to any other person or leaving anything where it may be found by, given to or brought to the attention of B or any other person,

(i) watching or spying on B or any other person,

(j) acting in any other way that a reasonable person would expect would cause B to suffer fear or alarm, and

'course of conduct' involves conduct on at least two occasions.

(7) A person convicted of the offence of stalking is liable—

(a) on conviction on indictment, to imprisonment for a term not exceeding 5 years, or to a fine, or to both,

(b) on summary conviction, to imprisonment for a term not exceeding 12 months, or to a fine not exceeding the statutory maximum, or to both.

(8) Subsection (9) applies where, in the trial of a person ('the accused') charged with the offence of stalking, the jury or, in summary proceedings, the court—

(a) is not satisfied that the accused committed the offence, but

(b) is satisfied that the accused committed an offence under section 38(1).

(9) The jury or, as the case may be, the court may acquit the accused of the charge and, instead, find the accused guilty of an offence under section 38(1).

[39A Offence of stalking committed outside the United Kingdom

(1) If—

(a) a person's course of conduct consists of or includes conduct in a country outside the United Kingdom,

(b) the course of conduct would constitute the offence of stalking if it occurred in Scotland, and

(c) the person is a United Kingdom national or is habitually resident in Scotland,

then the person commits that offence.

(2) If a person's course of conduct consists entirely of conduct in a country outside the United Kingdom—

(a) the person may be prosecuted, tried and punished for an offence of stalking by virtue of this section—

(i) in any sheriff court district in Scotland in which the person is apprehended or is in custody, or

(ii) in such sheriff court district as the Lord Advocate may determine,

as if the offence had been committed entirely in that district, and

(b) the offence is, for all purposes incidental to or consequential on trial or punishment, to be deemed to have been committed entirely in that district.

(3) In this section—

'country' includes territory;

'sheriff court district' is to be construed in accordance with section 307(1) of the Criminal Procedure (Scotland) Act 1995 (interpretation);

'United Kingdom national' means an individual who is—

(a) a British citizen, a British overseas territories citizen, a British National (Overseas) or a British Overseas citizen,

(b) a person who under the British Nationality Act 1981 is a British subject, or

(c) a British protected person within the meaning of that Act.]

BRIBERY ACT 2010
(2010, c 23)

General bribery offences

1 Offences of bribing another person

(1) A person ('P') is guilty of an offence if either of the following cases applies.

(2) Case 1 is where—

(a) P offers, promises or gives a financial or other advantage to another person, and

(b) P intends the advantage—

(i) to induce a person to perform improperly a relevant function or activity, or

(ii) to reward a person for the improper performance of such a function or activity.

(3) Case 2 is where—

(a) P offers, promises or gives a financial or other advantage to another person, and

(b) P knows or believes that the acceptance of the advantage would itself constitute the improper performance of a relevant function or activity.

(4) In case 1 it does not matter whether the person to whom the advantage is offered, promised or given is the same person as the person who is to perform, or has performed, the function or activity concerned.

(5) In cases 1 and 2 it does not matter whether the advantage is offered, promised or given by P directly or through a third party.

2 Offences relating to being bribed

(1) A person ('R') is guilty of an offence if any of the following cases applies.

(2) Case 3 is where R requests, agrees to receive or accepts a financial or other advantage intending that, in consequence, a relevant function or activity should be performed improperly (whether by R or another person).

(3) Anything that a person does (or omits to do) arising from or in connection with that person's past performance of a relevant function or activity is to be treated for the purposes of this Act as being done (or omitted) by that person in the performance of that function or activity.

5 Expectation test

(1) For the purposes of sections 3 and 4, the test of what is expected is a test of what a reasonable person in the United Kingdom would expect in relation to the performance of the type of function or activity concerned.

(2) In deciding what such a person would expect in relation to the performance of a function or activity where the performance is not subject to the law of any part of the United Kingdom, any local custom or practice is to be disregarded unless it is permitted or required by the written law applicable to the country or territory concerned.

(3) In subsection (2) 'written law' means law contained in—

(a) any written constitution, or provision made by or under legislation, applicable to the country or territory concerned, or

(b) any judicial decision which is so applicable and is evidenced in published written sources.

POLICE AND FIRE REFORM (SCOTLAND) ACT 2012 (2012, asp 8)

CHAPTER 15
OFFENCES

90 Assaulting or impeding police

(1) It is an offence for a person to assault—

(a) a person ('A') acting in a capacity mentioned in subsection (3), or

(b) a person assisting A while A is acting in such capacity.

(2) It is an offence for a person to resist, obstruct or hinder—

(a) a person ('A') acting in a capacity mentioned in subsection (3), or

(b) a person assisting A while A is acting in such capacity.

(3) The capacities are—

(a) that of a constable,

(b) that of a member of police staff,

(c) that of a member of a relevant police force when such member is executing a warrant or is otherwise acting in Scotland by virtue of any enactment conferring powers on the member in Scotland,

(d) that of a person who—

(i) is a member of an international joint investigation team that is led by a person acting in a capacity mentioned in paragraph (a) or (c), and

(ii) is carrying out functions as a member of that team.

(4) A person who is guilty of an offence under subsection (1) or (2) is liable on summary conviction to imprisonment for a period not exceeding 12 months or to a fine not exceeding the statutory maximum, or to both.

(5) A complaint may include a charge that is framed so as to comprise (in a combined form) the specification of both an offence under subsection (1) and an offence under subsection (2).

(6) Where a charge in a complaint is so framed the charge is to be regarded as being a single yet cumulative charge.

(7) In this section and section 91, a reference to a member of a relevant police force is a reference to a member of—

(a) a police force maintained under section 2 of the Police Act 1996 (c.16),

(b) the metropolitan police force,

(c) the City of London police force, or

(d) the Police Service of Northern Ireland.

91 Escape from custody

(1) It is an offence for a person—

(a) to remove a person from custody, or

(b) to assist the escape of a person in custody.

(2) The reference in subsection (1) to a person in custody is to be construed as a reference to a person—

(a) who is in the lawful custody of a person ('A') acting in a capacity mentioned in subsection (3) or a person assisting A while A is acting in such capacity, or

(b) who is in the act of eluding or escaping from such custody, whether or not the person has actually been arrested.

(3) The capacities are—

(a) that of a constable,

(b) that of a police custody and security officer,

(c) that of a member of a relevant police force when such member is executing a warrant or is otherwise acting in Scotland by virtue of any enactment conferring powers on the member in Scotland,

(d) that of a person who—

(i) is a member of an international joint investigation team that is led by a person acting in a capacity mentioned in paragraph (a) or (c), and

(ii) is carrying out functions as a member of that team.

(4) A person who is guilty of an offence under subsection (1) is liable on summary conviction to imprisonment for a period not exceeding 12 months or to a fine not exceeding the statutory maximum, or to both.

92 Impersonation etc.

(1) It is an offence for a person (not being a constable)—

(a) to impersonate a constable with an intent to deceive, or

(b) to do anything calculated to suggest that the person is a constable.

(2) It is an offence for a person (other than a constable) to possess any article of police uniform without the permission of the Authority.

(3) It is a defence for a person charged under subsection(2) to prove that the article—

(a) was obtained lawfully, and

(b) is in the person's possession for a lawful purpose.

(4) It is an offence for a person (other than a constable) to wear, without the prior permission of the Authority, any article of police uniform in circumstances where it gives an appearance so nearly resembling that of a constable as to be calculated to deceive.

(5) A person who is guilty of an offence under this section is liable on summary conviction to imprisonment for a period not exceeding 3 months or a fine not exceeding level 4 on the standard scale.

(6) In this section an 'article of police uniform' means—

(a) any article of uniform or any distinctive badge or mark usually issued to constables, or

(b) any article having the appearance of such article, badge or mark.

HUMAN TRAFFICKING AND EXPLOITATION (SCOTLAND) ACT 2015
(2015, asp 12)

PART 1
OFFENCES

Human trafficking

1 Offence of human trafficking

(1) A person commits an offence if the person—

(a) takes a relevant action, and

(b) does so with a view to another person being exploited.

(2) In this Part, 'relevant action' means an action which is any of the following—

(a) the recruitment of another person,

(b) the transportation or transfer of another person,

(c) the harbouring or receiving of another person,

(d) the exchange or transfer of control over another person, or

(e) the arrangement or facilitation of any of the actions mentioned in paragraphs (a) to (d).

(3) It is irrelevant whether the other person consents to any part of the relevant action.

(4) For the purposes of subsection (1), a person takes a relevant action with a view to another person being exploited only if—

(a) the person intends to exploit the other person (in any part of the world) during or after the relevant action, or

(b) the person knows or ought to know the other person is likely to be exploited (in any part of the world) during or after the relevant action.

(5) An offence under this section is to be known as the offence of human trafficking.

(6) A person who commits an offence of human trafficking is liable—

(a) on summary conviction, to imprisonment for a term not exceeding 12 months or a fine not exceeding the statutory maximum (or both),

(b) on conviction on indictment, to imprisonment for life or a fine (or both).

2 Application of offence to conduct in United Kingdom and elsewhere

(1) A person mentioned in subsection (2) commits an offence of human trafficking regardless of where the relevant action takes place.

(2) The persons are—

(a) a person who is a UK national,

(b) a person who at the time of the offence was habitually resident in Scotland,

(c) a body incorporated under the law of a part of the United Kingdom.

(3) A person not mentioned in subsection (2) commits an offence of human trafficking if—

(a) any part of the relevant action takes place in the United Kingdom, or

(b) the relevant action is taken with a view to a person arriving in or entering into, departing from, or travelling within, the United Kingdom.

3 Exploitation for purposes of offence of human trafficking

(1) For the purposes of section 1, a person is exploited only if one or more of the following subsections apply in relation to that person.

Slavery, servitude and forced or compulsory labour

(2) The person is the victim of conduct which—

(a) involves the commission of an offence under section 4, or

(b) would constitute such an offence were it done in Scotland.

Prostitution and sexual exploitation

(3) Another person exercises control, direction or influence over prostitution by the person in a way which shows that the other person is aiding, abetting or compelling the prostitution.

(4) Another person involves the person in the making or production of obscene or indecent material (material is to be construed in accordance with section 52(1)(a) of the Civic Government (Scotland) Act 1982 and includes images within the meaning of section 51A of that Act).

(5) The person is the victim of conduct which—

(a) involves the commission of an offence under—

(i) sections 1, 2 or 7 to 10 of the Criminal Law (Consolidation) (Scotland) Act 1995 (sexual offences),

(ii) sections 9 to 12 of the Protection of Children and Prevention of Sexual Offences (Scotland) Act 2005 (sexual services of children and child pornography),

(iii) Part 1 of the Sexual Offences (Scotland) Act 2009 (rape etc.),

(iv) Part 4 of the Sexual Offences (Scotland) Act 2009 (children), or

(v) Part 5 of the Sexual Offences (Scotland) Act 2009 (abuse of a position of trust), or

(b) would constitute such an offence were it done in Scotland.

Removal of organs etc.

(6) The person is encouraged, required or expected to do anything—

(a) which involves the commission, by the person or another person, of an offence under Part 1 of the Human Tissue (Scotland) Act 2006 (transplantation etc.),

(b) in connection with the removal of any part of a human body as a result of which the person or another person would commit an offence under the law of Scotland (other than an offence mentioned in paragraph (a)), or

(c) which would constitute an offence mentioned in paragraph (a) or (b) were it done in Scotland.

Securing services and benefits

(7) The person is subjected to force, threats or deception designed to induce the person—

(a) to provide services of any kind,

(b) to provide another person with benefits of any kind, or

(c) to enable another person to acquire benefits of any kind.

(8) Another person uses or attempts to use the person for any purpose within subsection (7)(a), (b) or (c), where—

(a) the person is—

(i) a child, or

(ii) an adult whose ability to refuse to be used for a purpose within subsection (7)(a), (b) or (c) is impaired through mental or physical illness, disability, old age or any other reason (a 'vulnerable adult'), and

(b) a person who is not a child or a vulnerable adult would be likely to refuse to be used for that purpose.

Slavery, servitude and forced or compulsory labour

4 Slavery, servitude and forced or compulsory labour

(1) A person commits an offence if—

(a) the person holds another person in slavery or servitude and the circumstances are such that the person knows or ought to know that the other person is so held, or

(b) the person requires another person to perform forced or compulsory labour and the circumstances are such that the person knows or ought to know that the other person is being required to perform such labour.

(2) In subsection (1) the references to holding a person in slavery or servitude or requiring a person to perform forced or compulsory labour are to be construed in accordance with Article 4 of the Human Rights Convention (which prohibits a person from being held in slavery or servitude or being required to perform forced or compulsory labour).

(3) In determining whether a person is being held in slavery or servitude or required to perform forced or compulsory labour, regard is to be had in particular to any personal circumstances of the person (for example the person being a child, or the person's age, or the person's family relationships

or health) that may make the person more vulnerable than other persons.

(4) The consent of a person to any of the acts alleged to constitute holding the person in slavery or servitude or requiring the person to perform forced or compulsory labour, does not preclude a determination that the person is being held in slavery or servitude or required to perform forced or compulsory labour.

(5) A person who commits an offence under this section is liable—

(a) on summary conviction, to imprisonment for a term not exceeding 12 months or a fine not exceeding the statutory maximum (or both),

(b) on conviction on indictment, to imprisonment for life or a fine (or both).

(6) In this section 'the Human Rights Convention' means the Convention for the Protection of Human Rights and Fundamental Freedoms agreed by the Council of Europe at Rome on 4 November 1950.

ABUSIVE BEHAVIOUR AND SEXUAL HARM (SCOTLAND) ACT 2016
(2016, asp 22)

PART 1
ABUSIVE BEHAVIOUR

Abusive behaviour towards partner or ex-partner

1 Aggravation of offence where abuse of partner or ex-partner

(1) This subsection applies where it is—

(a) libelled in an indictment or specified in a complaint that an offence is aggravated by involving abuse of the partner or ex-partner of the person committing it, and

(b) proved that the offence is so aggravated.

(2) An offence is aggravated as described in subsection (1)(a) if in committing the offence—

(a) the person intends to cause the partner or ex-partner to suffer physical or psychological harm, or

(b) in the case only of an offence committed against the partner or ex-partner, the person is reckless as to causing the partner or ex-partner to suffer physical or psychological harm.

(3) It is immaterial for the purposes of subsection (2) that the offence does not in fact cause the partner or ex-partner physical or psychological harm.

(4) Evidence from a single source is sufficient to prove that an offence is aggravated as described in subsection (1)(a).

(5) Where subsection (1) applies, the court must—

(a) state on conviction that the offence is aggravated as described in subsection (1)(a),

(b) record the conviction in a way that shows that the offence is so aggravated,

(c) take the aggravation into account in determining the appropriate sentence, and

(d) state—

(i) where the sentence imposed in respect of the offence is different from that which the court would have imposed if the offence were not so aggravated, the extent of and the reasons for that difference, or

(ii) otherwise, the reasons for there being no such difference.

(6) For the purposes of this section, a person is a partner of another person if they are—

(a) spouses or civil partners of each other,

(b) living together as if spouses [...] of each other, or

(c) in an intimate personal relationship with each other,

and the references to a person's ex-partner are to be construed accordingly.

(7) In this section—

'cause' includes contribute to causing (and 'causing' is to be construed accordingly),

'psychological harm' includes fear, alarm or distress.

Disclosure of an intimate photograph or film

2 Disclosing, or threatening to disclose, an intimate photograph or film

(1) A person ('A') commits an offence if—

(a) A discloses, or threatens to disclose, a photograph or film which shows, or appears to show, another person ('B') in an intimate situation,

(b) by doing so, A intends to cause B fear, alarm or distress or A is reckless as to whether B will be caused fear, alarm or distress, and

(c) the photograph or film has not previously been disclosed to the public at large, or any section of the public, by B or with B's consent.

(2) For the purposes of this section, a photograph or film is disclosed if it, or any data or other thing which is capable of being converted into it, is given, shown or made available to a person other than B.

(3) In proceedings for an offence under subsection (1), A has a defence if any of the following facts is established—

(a) B consented to the photograph or film being disclosed,

(b) A reasonably believed that B consented to the photograph or film being disclosed,

(c) A reasonably believed that disclosure of the photograph or film was necessary for the purposes of the prevention, detection, investigation or prosecution of crime, or

(d) A reasonably believed that disclosure of the photograph or film was in the public interest.

(4) For the purposes of subsection (3), consent to the photograph or film being disclosed may be—

(a) consent which is specific to the particular disclosure or (as the case may be) the particular threatened disclosure, or

(b) consent to disclosure generally where that consent covers the particular disclosure or (as the case may be) the particular threatened disclosure.

(5) In proceedings for an offence under subsection (1), A has a defence if the following matter is established—

(a) B was in the intimate situation shown in the photograph or film,

(b) B was not in the intimate situation as a result of a deliberate act of another person to which B did not agree, and

(c) when B was in the intimate situation—

(i) B was in a place to which members of the public had access (whether or not on payment of a fee), and

(ii) members of the public were present.

(6) For the purposes of subsection (3), a fact is established, and for the purposes of subsection (5), the matter is established, if—

(a) sufficient evidence is adduced to raise an issue as to whether that is the case, and

(b) the prosecution does not prove beyond reasonable doubt that it is not the case.

(7) A person who commits an offence under subsection (1) is liable—

(a) on summary conviction, to imprisonment for a term not exceeding 12 months or a fine not exceeding the statutory maximum (or both),

(b) on conviction on indictment, to imprisonment for a term not exceeding 5 years or a fine (or both).

CRIMINAL JUSTICE (SCOTLAND) ACT 2016
(2016, asp 1)

PART 1
ARREST AND CUSTODY

CHAPTER 1
ARREST BY POLICE

1 Power of a constable

(1) A constable may arrest a person without a warrant if the constable has reasonable grounds for suspecting that the person has committed or is committing an offence.

(2) In relation to an offence not punishable by imprisonment, a constable may arrest a person under subsection (1) only if the constable is satisfied that it would not be in the interests of justice to delay the arrest in order to seek a warrant for the person's arrest.

(3) Without prejudice to the generality of subsection (2), it would not be in the interests of justice to delay an arrest in order to seek a warrant if the constable reasonably believes that unless the person is arrested without delay the person will—

(a) continue committing the offence, or

(b) obstruct the course of justice in any way, including by—

(i) seeking to avoid arrest, or

(ii) interfering with witnesses or evidence.

(4) For the avoidance of doubt, an offence is to be regarded as not punishable by imprisonment for the purpose of subsection (2) only if no person convicted of the offence can be sentenced to imprisonment in respect of it.

2 Exercise of the power

(1) A person may be arrested under section 1 more than once in respect of the same offence.

(2) A person may not be arrested under section 1 in respect of an offence if the person has been officially accused of

committing the offence or an offence arising from the same circumstances as the offence.

(3) Where—

(a) a constable who is not in uniform arrests a person under section 1, and

(b) the person asks to see the constable's identification,

the constable must show identification to the person as soon as reasonably practicable.

3 Information to be given on arrest

When a constable arrests a person (or as soon afterwards as is reasonably practicable), a constable must inform the person—

(a) that the person is under arrest,

(b) of the general nature of the offence in respect of which the person is arrested [(if any)],

(c) of the reason for the arrest,

(d) that the person is under no obligation to say anything, other than to give the information specified in section 34(4), and

(e) of the person's right to have—

(i) intimation sent to a solicitor under section 43, and

(ii) access to a solicitor under section 44.

4 Arrested person to be taken to police station

(1) Where a person is arrested by a constable outwith a police station, a constable must take the person as quickly as is reasonably practicable to a police station.

[(1A) But subsection (1) need not be complied with if—

(a) either the warrant under which the person was arrested or an enactment requires that following the arrest the person be taken to a particular place (other than a police station), and

(b) the taking of the person to that place would be unnecessarily delayed by taking the person to a police station first.]

(2) Subsection (1) ceases to apply, and the person must be released from police custody immediately, if—

(a) the person has been arrested [in respect of an offence] without a warrant,

(b) the person has not yet arrived at a police station in accordance with this section, and

(c) in the opinion of a constable there are no reasonable grounds for suspecting that the person has committed—

(i) the offence in respect of which the person was arrested, or

(ii) an offence arising from the same circumstances as that offence.

(3) For the avoidance of doubt, subsection (1) ceases to apply if, before arriving at a police station in accordance with this section, the person is released from custody under—

(a) section 25(2), or

(b) section 28(3A) of the 1995 Act.

5 Information to be given at police station

(1) Subsections (2) and (3) apply when—

(a) a person is in police custody having been arrested at a police station, or

(b) a person is in police custody and has been taken to a police station in accordance with section 4.

(2) The person must be informed as soon as reasonably practicable—

(a) that the person is under no obligation to say anything, other than to give the information specified in section 34(4),

(b) of any right the person has to have intimation sent and to have access to certain persons under—

(i) section 38,

(ii) section 40,

(iii) section 43,

(iv) section 44.

(3) The person must be provided as soon as reasonably practicable with such information (verbally or in writing) as is necessary to satisfy the [requirements placed on member States by] Articles 3 and 4 of Directive 2012/13/EU of the

European Parliament and of the Council on the right to information in criminal proceedings.

6 Information to be recorded by police

(1) There must be recorded in relation to any arrest by a constable—

(a) the time and place of arrest,

[(b) either—

(i) the general nature of the offence in respect of which the person is arrested, or

(ii) if the person is arrested otherwise than in respect of an offence, the reason for the arrest,]

(c) if the person is taken from one place to another while in police custody (including to a police station in accordance with section 4)—

(i) the place from which, and time at which, the person is taken, and

(ii) the place to which the person is taken and the time at which the person arrives there,

(d) the time at which, and the identity of the constable by whom, the person is informed of the matters mentioned in section 3,

(e) the time at which the person ceases to be in police custody.

(2) Where relevant, there must be recorded in relation to an arrest by a constable—

(a) the reason that the constable who released the person from custody under subsection (2) of section 4 formed the opinion mentioned in paragraph (c) of that subsection,

(b) the time at which, and the identity of the person by whom, the person is—

(i) informed of the matters mentioned in subsection (2) of section 5, and

(ii) provided with information in accordance with subsection (3) of that section,

(c) the time at which, and the identity of the person by whom, the person is informed of the matters mentioned in section 20,

(d) the time at which the person requests that intimation be sent under—

(i) section 38,

(ii) section 43,

(e) the time at which intimation is sent under—

(i) section 38,

(ii) section 41,

(iii) section 42,

(iv) section 43.

(3) Where a person is in police custody and not officially accused of committing an offence, there must be recorded the time, place and outcome of any decision under section 7.

(4) Where a person is held in police custody by virtue of authorisation given under section 7 there must be recorded—

(a) the time at which the person is informed of the matters mentioned in section 8,

(b) the time, place and outcome of any custody review under section 13,

(c) the time at which any interview in the circumstances described in section 15(6) begins and the time at which it ends.

(5) If a constable considers whether to give authorisation under section 11 there must be recorded—

(a) whether a reasonable opportunity to make representations has been afforded in accordance with subsection (4)(a) of that section,

(b) if the opportunity referred to in paragraph (a) has not been afforded, the reason for that,

(c) the time, place and outcome of the constable's decision, and

(d) if the constable's decision is to give the authorisation—

(i) the grounds on which it is given,

(ii) the time at which, and the identity of the person by whom, the person is informed and reminded of things in accordance with section 12, and

(iii) the time at which the person requests that intimation be sent under section 12(3)(a) and the time at which it is sent.

(6) Where a person is held in police custody by virtue of authorisation given under section 11 there must be recorded—

(a) the time, place and outcome of any custody review under section 13,

(b) the time at which any interview in the circumstances described in section 15(6) begins and the time at which it ends.

(7) If a person is released from police custody on conditions under section 16, there must be recorded—

(a) details of the conditions imposed, and

(b) the identity of the constable who imposed them.

(8) If a person is charged with an offence by a constable while in police custody, there must be recorded the time at which the person is charged.

CHAPTER 2
CUSTODY: PERSON NOT OFFICIALLY ACCUSED

Keeping person in custody

7 Authorisation for keeping in custody

(1) Subsection (2) applies where—

(a) a person is in police custody having been arrested [in respect of an offence] without a warrant, and

(b) since being arrested, the person has not been charged with an offence by a constable.

(2) Authorisation to keep the person in custody must be sought as soon as reasonably practicable after the person—

(a) is arrested at a police station, or

(b) arrives at a police station, having been taken there in accordance with section 4.

(3) Authorisation may be given only by a constable who—

(a) is of the rank of sergeant or above, and

(b) has not been involved in the investigation in connection with which the person is in police custody.

(4) Authorisation may be given only if that constable is satisfied that the test in section 14 is met.

(5) If authorisation is refused, the person may continue to be held in police custody only if—

(a) a constable charges the person with an offence, or

(b) the person is detained under section 28(1A) of the 1995 Act (which allows for detention in connection with a breach of bail conditions).

8 Information to be given on authorisation

At the time when authorisation to keep a person in custody is given under section 7, the person must be informed of—

(a) the reason that the person is being kept in custody, and

(b) the 12 hour limit arising by virtue of section 9 and the fact that the person may be kept in custody for a further 12 hours under section 11.

9 12 hour limit: general rule

(1) Subsection (2) applies when—

(a) a person has been held in police custody for a continuous period of 12 hours, beginning with the time at which authorisation was given under section 7, and

(b) during that period the person has not been charged with an offence by a constable.

(2) The person may continue to be held in police custody only if—

(a) a constable charges the person with an offence,

(b) authorisation to keep the person in custody has been given under section 11, or

(c) the person is detained under section 28(1A) of the 1995 Act (which allows for detention in connection with a breach of bail conditions).

10 12 hour limit: previous period

(1) Subsection (2) applies where—

(a) a person is being held in police custody by virtue of authorisation given under section 7,

(b) authorisation has been given under that section to hold the person in police custody on a previous occasion, and

(c) the offence in connection with which the authorisation mentioned in paragraph (a) has been given is the same offence or arises from the same circumstances as the offence in connection with which the authorisation mentioned in paragraph (b) was given.

(2) The 12 hour period mentioned in section 9 is reduced by the length of the period during which the person was held in police custody by virtue of the authorisation mentioned in subsection (1)(b).

(3) Subsections (5) and (6) of section 15 apply for the purpose of calculating the length of the period during which the person was held in police custody by virtue of the authorisation mentioned in subsection (1)(b).

11 Authorisation for keeping in custody beyond 12 hour limit

(1) A constable may give authorisation for a person who is in police custody to be kept in custody for a continuous period of 12 hours, beginning when the 12 hour period mentioned in section 9 ends.

(2) Authorisation may be given only by a constable who—

(a) is of, or above, the rank of—

(i) inspector, if a constable believes the person to be 18 years of age or over,

(ii) chief inspector, if a constable believes the person to be under 18 years of age, and

(b) has not been involved in the investigation in connection with which the person is in police custody.

(3) Authorisation may be given only if—

(a) the person has not been held in police custody by virtue of authorisation given under this section in connection with—

(i) the offence in connection with which the person is in police custody, or

(ii) an offence arising from the same circumstances as that offence, and

(b) the constable is satisfied that—

(i) the test in section 14 will be met when the 12 hour period mentioned in section 9 ends,

(ii) the offence in connection with which the person is in police custody is an indictable offence, and

(iii) the investigation is being conducted diligently and expeditiously.

(4) Before deciding whether or not to give authorisation the constable must—

(a) where practicable afford a reasonable opportunity to make verbal or written representations to—

(i) the person, or

(ii) if the person so chooses, the person's solicitor, and

(b) have regard to any representations made.

(5) If authorisation is given, it is deemed to be withdrawn if the person is released from police custody before the 12 hour period mentioned in section 9 ends.

(6) Subsection (7) applies when—

(a) by virtue of authorisation given under this section, a person has been held in police custody for a continuous period of 12 hours (beginning with the time at which the 12 hour period mentioned in section 9 ended), and

(b) during that period the person has not been charged with an offence by a constable.

(7) The person may continue to be held in police custody only if—

(a) a constable charges the person with an offence, or

(b) the person is detained under section 28(1A) of the 1995 Act (which allows for detention in connection with a breach of bail conditions).

12 Information to be given on authorisation under section 11

(1) This section applies when authorisation to keep a person in custody is given under section 11.

(2) The person must be informed—

(a) that the authorisation has been given, and

(b) of the grounds on which it has been given.

(3) The person—

(a) has the right to have the information mentioned in subsection (2) intimated to a solicitor, and

(b) must be informed of that right.

(4) The person must be reminded about any right which the person has under Chapter 5.

(5) Subsection (4) does not require that a person be reminded about a right to have intimation sent under either of the following sections if the person has exercised the right already—

(a) section 38,

(b) section 43.

(6) Information to be given under subsections (2), (3)(b) and (4) must be given to the person as soon as reasonably practicable after the authorisation is given.

(7) Where the person requests that intimation be sent under subsection (3)(a), the intimation must be sent as soon as reasonably practicable.

13 Custody review

(1) A custody review must be carried out—

(a) when a person has been held in police custody for a continuous period of 6 hours by virtue of authorisation given under section 7, and

(b) again, if authorisation to keep the person in police custody is given under section 11, when the person has been held in custody for a continuous period of 6 hours by virtue of that authorisation.

(2) A custody review entails the consideration by a constable of whether the test in section 14 is met.

(3) A custody review must be carried out by a constable who—

(a) is of the rank of inspector or above, and

(b) has not been involved in the investigation in connection with which the person is in police custody.

(4) If the constable is not satisfied that the test in section 14 is met, the person may continue to be held in police custody only if—

(a) a constable charges the person with an offence, or

(b) the person is detained under section 28(1A) of the 1995 Act (which allows for detention in connection with a breach of bail conditions).

14 Test for sections 7, 11 and 13

(1) For the purposes of sections 7(4), 11(3)(b) and 13(2), the test is that—

(a) there are reasonable grounds for suspecting that the person has committed an offence, and

(b) keeping the person in custody is necessary and proportionate for the purposes of bringing the person before a court or otherwise dealing with the person in accordance with the law.

(2) Without prejudice to the generality of subsection (1)(b), in considering what is necessary and proportionate for the purpose mentioned in that subsection regard may be had to—

(a) whether the person's presence is reasonably required to enable the offence to be investigated fully,

(b) whether the person (if liberated) would be likely to interfere with witnesses or evidence, or otherwise obstruct the course of justice,

(c) the nature and seriousness of the offence.

15 Medical treatment

(1) Subsection (2) applies when—

(a) a person is in police custody having been arrested without a warrant,

(b) since being arrested, the person has not been charged with an offence by a constable, and

(c) the person is at a hospital for the purpose of receiving medical treatment.

(2) If authorisation to keep the person in custody has not been given under section 7, that section has effect as if—

(a) each reference in subsection (2) of that section to a police station were a reference to the hospital, and

(b) the words after the reference to a police station in paragraph (b) of that subsection were omitted.

(3) Where authorisation is given under section 7 when a person is at a hospital, authorisation under that section need not be sought again if, while still in custody, the person is taken to a police station in accordance with section 4.

(4) Subsections (5) and (6) apply for the purpose of calculating the 12 hours mentioned in sections 9 and 11.

(5) Except as provided for in subsection (6), no account is to be taken of any period during which a person is—

(a) at a hospital for the purpose of receiving medical treatment, or

(b) being taken as quickly as is reasonably practicable—

(i) to a hospital for the purpose of receiving medical treatment, or

(ii) to a police station from a hospital to which the person was taken for the purpose of receiving medical treatment.

(6) Account is to be taken of any period during which a person is both—

(a) at a hospital, or being taken to or from one, and

(b) being interviewed by a constable in relation to an offence which the constable has reasonable grounds to suspect the person of committing.

Investigative liberation

16 Release on conditions

(1) Subsection (2) applies where—

(a) a person is being held in police custody by virtue of authorisation given under section 7,

(b) a constable has reasonable grounds for suspecting that the person has committed a relevant offence, and

(c) either—

(i) the person has not been subject to a condition imposed under subsection (2) in connection with a relevant offence, or

(ii) it has not been more than 28 days since the first occasion on which a condition was imposed on the person under subsection (2) in connection with a relevant offence.

(2) If releasing the person from custody, a constable may impose any condition that an appropriate constable considers necessary and proportionate for the purpose of ensuring the proper conduct of the investigation into a relevant offence (including, for example, a condition aimed at securing that the person does not interfere with witnesses or evidence).

(3) A condition under subsection (2)—

(a) may not require the person to be in a specified place at a specified time,

(b) may require the person—

(i) not to be in a specified place, or category of place, at a specified time, and

(ii) to remain outwith that place, or any place falling within the specified category (if any), for a specified period.

(4) A condition imposed under subsection (2) is a liberation condition for the purposes of schedule 1.

(5) In subsection (2), 'an appropriate constable' means a constable of the rank of sergeant or above.

(6) In this section, 'a relevant offence' means—

(a) the offence in connection with which the authorisation under section 7 has been given, or

(b) an offence arising from the same circumstances as that offence.

17 Conditions ceasing to apply

(1) A condition imposed on a person under section 16(2) ceases to apply—

(a) at the end of the day falling 28 days after the first occasion on which a condition was imposed on the person under section 16(2) in connection with a relevant offence, or

(b) before then, if—

(i) the condition is removed by a notice under section 18,

(ii) the person is arrested in connection with a relevant offence,

(iii) the person is officially accused of committing a relevant offence, or

(iv) the condition is removed by the sheriff under section 19.

(2) In subsection (1), 'a relevant offence' means—

(a) the offence in connection with which the condition was imposed, or

(b) an offence arising from the same circumstances as that offence.

18 Modification or removal of conditions

(1) A constable may by notice modify or remove a condition imposed under section 16(2).

(2) A notice under subsection (1)—

(a) is to be given in writing to the person who is subject to the condition,

(b) must specify the time from which the condition is modified or removed.

(3) A constable of the rank of inspector or above must keep under review whether or not—

(a) there are reasonable grounds for suspecting that a person who is subject to a condition imposed under section 16(2) has committed a relevant offence, and

(b) the condition imposed remains necessary and proportionate for the purpose of ensuring the proper conduct of the investigation into a relevant offence.

(4) Where the constable referred to in subsection (3) is no longer satisfied as to the matter mentioned in paragraph (a) of that subsection, a constable must give notice to the person

removing any condition imposed in connection with a relevant offence.

(5) Where the constable referred to in subsection (3) is no longer satisfied as to the matter mentioned in paragraph (b) of that subsection, a constable must give notice to the person—

(a) modifying the condition in question, or

(b) removing it.

(6) Where a duty to give notice to a person arises under subsection (4) or (5), the notice—

(a) is to be given in writing to the person as soon as practicable, and

(b) must specify, as the time from which the condition is modified or removed, the time at which the duty to give the notice arose.

(7) The modification or removal of a condition under subsection (1), (4) or (5) requires the authority of a constable of the rank of inspector or above.

(8) In this section, 'a relevant offence' means—

(a) the offence in connection with which the condition was imposed, or

(b) an offence arising from the same circumstances as that offence.

19 Review of conditions

(1) A person who is subject to a condition imposed under section 16(2) may apply to the sheriff to have the condition reviewed.

(2) Before disposing of an application under this section, the sheriff must give the procurator fiscal an opportunity to make representations.

(3) If the sheriff is not satisfied that the condition is necessary and proportionate for the purpose for which it was imposed, the sheriff may—

(a) remove the condition, or

(b) impose an alternative condition that the sheriff considers to be necessary and proportionate for that purpose.

(4) For the purposes of sections 17 and 18, a condition imposed by the sheriff under subsection (3)(b) is to be regarded as having been imposed under section 16(2).

CHAPTER 3
CUSTODY: PERSON OFFICIALLY ACCUSED

Person to be brought before court

20 [Information to be given in particular cases]

(1) Subsection (2) applies when—

(a) a person is in police custody having been arrested under a warrant in respect of [an offence listed in subsection (3)(b)], or

(b) a person—

(i) is in police custody having been arrested without a warrant, and

(ii) since being arrested, the person has been charged by a constable with [an offence listed in subsection (3)(b)].

(2) The person must be informed as soon as reasonably practicable—

(a) that the person's case at, or for the purposes of, any relevant hearing [...] in the course of the proceedings may be conducted only by a lawyer,

(b) that it is, therefore, in the person's interests to get the professional assistance of a solicitor, and

(c) that if the person does not engage a solicitor for the purposes of the conduct of the person's case at or for the purposes of the hearing, the court will do so.

[(3) For the purposes of subsections (1) and (2)—

(a) 'relevant hearing' is to be construed in accordance with section 288C(1A) or (as the case may be) 288DC(4) of the 1995 Act,

(b) the list is—

(i) an offence to which section 288C of the 1995 Act applies (certain sexual offending),

(ii) an offence to which section 288DC of the 1995 Act applies (domestic abuse cases).]

21 Person to be brought before court

(1) Subsection (2) applies to a person when—

(a) the person is in police custody having been arrested under a warrant [granted for the purpose of having the person brought before a court in connection with an offence which the person is officially accused of committing], or

(b) the person—

(i) is in police custody having been arrested [in respect of an offence] without a warrant, and

(ii) since being arrested, the person has been charged with an offence by a constable.

(2) The person must be brought before a court (unless released from custody under section 25)—

(a) if practicable, before the end of the first day on which the court is sitting after the day on which this subsection began to apply to the person, or

(b) as soon as practicable after that.

(3) A person is deemed to be brought before a court in accordance with subsection (2) if the person appears before it by means of a live television link (by virtue of a determination by the court that the person is to do so by such means).

22 Under 18s to be kept in place of safety prior to court

(1) Subsection (2) applies when—

(a) a person is to be brought before a court in accordance with section 21(2), and

[(b) a constable believes the person is under 18 years of age.]

(2) The person must (unless released from custody under section 25) be kept in a place of safety until the person can be brought before the court.

(3) The place of safety in which the person is kept must not be a police station unless an appropriate constable certifies that keeping the person in a place of safety other than a police station would be—

(a) impracticable,

(b) unsafe, or

(c) inadvisable due to the person's state of health (physical or mental).

(4) A certificate under subsection (3) must be produced to the court when the person is brought before it.

(5) In this section—

'an appropriate constable' means a constable of the rank of inspector or above,

'place of safety' has the meaning given in section 202(1) of the Children's Hearings (Scotland) Act 2011.

23 Notice to parent that under 18 to be brought before court

(1) Subsection (2) applies when a person who is [under 18] years of age—

(a) is to be brought before a court in accordance with section 21(2), or

(b) is released from police custody on an undertaking given under section 25(2)(a).

(2) A parent of the person mentioned in subsection (1) (if one can be found) must be informed of the following matters—

(a) the court before which the person is to be brought,

(b) the date on which the person is to be brought before the court,

(c) the general nature of the offence which the person has been officially accused of committing, and

(d) that the parent's attendance at the court may be required under section 42 of the 1995 Act.

(3) Subsection (2) does not require any information to be given to a parent if a constable has grounds to believe that giving the parent the information mentioned in that subsection may be detrimental to the wellbeing of the person mentioned in subsection (1).

(4) In this section—

'parent' includes guardian and any person who has the care of the person mentioned in subsection (1),

[...]

24 Notice to local authority that under 18 to be brought before court

(1) The appropriate local authority must be informed of the matters mentioned in subsection (4) when—

(a) a person to whom [subsection (2)] applies is to be brought before a court in accordance with section 21(2), or

(b) a person to whom subsection (2) applies is released from police custody on an undertaking given under section 25(2)(a).

[(2) This subsection applies to a person who is under 18 years of age.]

(3) […]

(4) The matters referred to in subsection (1) are—

(a) the court before which the person mentioned in paragraph (a) or (as the case may be) (b) of that subsection is to be brought,

(b) the date on which the person is to be brought before the court, and

(c) the general nature of the offence which the person has been officially accused of committing.

(5) For the purpose of subsection (1), the appropriate local authority is the local authority in whose area the court referred to in subsection (4)(a) sits.

Police liberation

25 Liberation by police

(1) Subsection (2) applies when—

(a) a person is in police custody having been arrested under a warrant (other than a warrant granted under section 37(1)), or

(b) a person—

(i) is in police custody having been arrested without a warrant, and

(ii) since being arrested, the person has been charged with an offence by a constable.

(2) A constable may—

(a) if the person gives an undertaking in accordance with section 26, release the person from custody,

(b) release the person from custody without such an undertaking,

(c) refuse to release the person from custody.

(3) Where a person is in custody as mentioned in subsection (1)(a), the person may not be released from custody under subsection (2)(b).

(4) A constable is not to be subject to any claim whatsoever by reason of having refused to release a person from custody under subsection (2)(c).

26 Release on undertaking

(1) A person may be released from police custody on an undertaking given under section 25(2)(a) only if the person signs the undertaking.

(2) The terms of an undertaking are that the person undertakes to—

(a) appear at a specified court at a specified time, and

(b) comply with any conditions imposed under subsection (3) while subject to the undertaking.

(3) The conditions which may be imposed under this subsection are—

(a) that the person does not—

(i) commit an offence,

(ii) interfere with witnesses or evidence, or otherwise obstruct the course of justice,

(iii) behave in a manner which causes, or is likely to cause, alarm or distress to witnesses,

(b) any further condition that a constable considers necessary and proportionate for the purpose of ensuring that any conditions imposed under paragraph (a) are observed.

(4) Conditions which may be imposed under subsection (3)(b) include—

(a) a condition requiring the person—

(i) to be in a specified place at a specified time, and

(ii) to remain there for a specified period,

(b) a condition requiring the person—

(i) not to be in a specified place, or category of place, at a specified time, and

(ii) to remain outwith that place, or any place falling within the specified category (if any), for a specified period.

(5) For the imposition of a condition under subsection (3)(b)—

(a) if it is of the kind described in subsection (4)(a), the authority of a constable of the rank of inspector or above is required,

(b) if it is of any other kind, the authority of a constable of the rank of sergeant or above is required.

(6) The requirements imposed by an undertaking to attend at a court and comply with conditions are liberation conditions for the purposes of schedule 1.

27 Modification of undertaking

(1) The procurator fiscal may by notice modify the terms of an undertaking given under section 25(2)(a) by—

(a) changing the court specified as the court at which the person is to appear,

(b) changing the time specified as the time at which the person is to appear at the court,

(c) removing or altering any condition imposed under section 26(3).

(2) A condition may not be altered under subsection (1)(c) so as to forbid or require something not forbidden or required by the terms of the condition when the person gave the undertaking.

(3) Notice under subsection (1) must be effected in a manner by which citation may be effected under section 141 of the 1995 Act.

28 Rescission of undertaking

(1) The procurator fiscal may by notice rescind an undertaking given under section 25(2)(a) (whether or not the person who gave it is to be prosecuted).

(2) The rescission of an undertaking by virtue of subsection (1) takes effect at the end of the day on which the notice is sent.

(3) Notice under subsection (1) must be effected in a manner by which citation may be effected under section 141 of the 1995 Act.

(4) A constable may arrest a person without a warrant if the constable has reasonable grounds for suspecting that the person is likely to fail to comply with the terms of an undertaking given under section 25(2)(a).

(5) Where a person is arrested under subsection (4) or subsection (6) applies—

(a) the undertaking referred to in subsection (4) or (as the case may be) (6) is rescinded, and

(b) this Part applies as if the person, since being most recently arrested, has been charged with the offence in connection with which the person was in police custody when the undertaking was given.

(6) This subsection applies where—

(a) a person who is subject to an undertaking given under section 25(2)(a) is in police custody (otherwise than as a result of having been arrested under subsection (4)), and

(b) a constable has reasonable grounds for suspecting that the person has failed, or (if liberated) is likely to fail, to comply with the terms of the undertaking.

(7) The references in subsections (4) and (6)(b) to the terms of the undertaking are to the terms of the undertaking subject to any modification by—

(a) notice under section 27(1), or

(b) the sheriff under section 30(3)(b).

29 Expiry of undertaking

(1) An undertaking given under section 25(2)(a) expires—

(a) at the end of the day on which the person who gave it is required by its terms to appear at a court, or

(b) if subsection (2) applies, at the end of the day on which the person who gave it is brought before a court having been arrested under the warrant mentioned in that subsection.

(2) This subsection applies where—

(a) a person fails to appear at court as required by the terms of an undertaking given under section 25(2)(a), and

(b) on account of that failure, a warrant for the person's arrest is granted.

(3) The references in subsections (1)(a) and (2)(a) to the terms of the undertaking are to the terms of the undertaking subject to any modification by notice under section 27(1).

30 Review of undertaking

(1) A person who is subject to an undertaking containing a condition imposed under section 26(3)(b) may apply to the sheriff to have the condition reviewed.

(2) Before disposing of an application under this section, the sheriff must give the procurator fiscal an opportunity to make representations.

(3) If the sheriff is not satisfied that the condition is necessary and proportionate for the purpose for which it was imposed, the sheriff may modify the terms of the undertaking by—

(a) removing the condition, or

(b) imposing an alternative condition that the sheriff considers to be necessary and proportionate for that purpose.

CHAPTER 4
POLICE INTERVIEW

Rights of suspects

31 Information to be given before interview

(1) Subsection (2) applies to a person who—

(a) is in police custody, or

(b) is attending at a police station or other place voluntarily for the purpose of being interviewed by a constable.

(2) Not more than one hour before a constable interviews the person about an offence which the constable has

reasonable grounds to suspect the person of committing, the person must be informed—

(a) of the general nature of that offence,

(b) that the person is under no obligation to say anything other than to give the information specified in section 34(4),

(c) about the right under section 32 to have a solicitor present during the interview, and

(d) if the person is in police custody, about any right which the person has under Chapter 5.

(3) A person need not be informed under subsection (2)(d) about a right to have intimation sent under either of the following sections if the person has exercised the right already—

(a) section 38,

(b) section 43.

(4) For the purpose of subsection (2), a constable is not to be regarded as interviewing a person about an offence merely by asking the person for the information specified in section 34(4).

(5) Where a person is to be interviewed by virtue of authorisation granted under section 35, before the interview begins the person must be informed of what was specified by the court under subsection (6) of that section.

32 Right to have solicitor present

(1) Subsections (2) and (3) apply to a person who—

(a) is in police custody, or

(b) is attending at a police station or other place voluntarily for the purpose of being interviewed by a constable.

(2) The person has the right to have a solicitor present while being interviewed by a constable about an offence which the constable has reasonable grounds to suspect the person of committing.

(3) Accordingly—

(a) unless the person consents to being interviewed without having a solicitor present, a constable must not begin to interview the person about the offence until the person's solicitor is present, and

(b) the person's solicitor must not be denied access to the person at any time while a constable is interviewing the person about the offence.

(4) Despite subsection (3)(a) a constable may, in exceptional circumstances, proceed to interview the person without a solicitor being present if it is necessary to interview the person without delay in the interests of—

(a) the investigation or the prevention of crime, or

(b) the apprehension of offenders.

(5) A decision to allow the person to be interviewed without a solicitor present by virtue of subsection (4) may be taken only by a constable who—

(a) is of the rank of sergeant or above, and

(b) has not been involved in investigating the offence about which the person is to be interviewed.

(6) For the purposes of subsections (2) and (3), a constable is not to be regarded as interviewing a person about an offence merely by asking the person for the information specified in section 34(4).

(7) Where a person consents to being interviewed without having a solicitor present, there must be recorded—

(a) the time at which the person consented, and

(b) any reason given by the person at that time for waiving the right to have a solicitor present.

33 Consent to interview without solicitor

(1) [Subsection (2) applies] for the purpose of section 32(3)(a).

(2) A person may not consent to being interviewed without having a solicitor present if—

(a) the person is under [18] years of age

(b) [...]

(c) the person is [18] years of age or over and, owing to mental disorder, appears to a constable to be unable to—

(i) understand sufficiently what is happening, or

(ii) communicate effectively with the police.

(3) [...]

(4) […]
(5) […]
(6) In subsection (2)(c)—
(a) 'mental disorder' has the meaning given by section 328 of the Mental Health (Care and Treatment) (Scotland) Act 2003,
(b) the reference to the police is to any—
(i) constable, or
(ii) person appointed as a member of police staff under section 26(1) of the Police and Fire Reform (Scotland) Act 2012.

Person not officially accused

34 Questioning following arrest

(1) Subsections (2) and (4) apply where—
(a) a person is in police custody in relation to an offence, and
(b) the person has not been officially accused of committing the offence or an offence arising from the same circumstances as the offence.
(2) A constable may put questions to the person in relation to the offence.
(3) For the avoidance of doubt, nothing in this section is to be taken to mean that a constable cannot put questions to the person in relation to any other matter.
(4) The person is under no obligation to answer any question, other than to give the following information—
(a) the person's name,
(b) the person's address,
(c) the person's date of birth,
(d) the person's place of birth (in such detail as a constable considers necessary or expedient for the purpose of establishing the person's identity), and
(e) the person's nationality.
(5) Subsection (2) is without prejudice to any rule of law as regards the admissibility in evidence of any answer given.

Person officially accused

35 Authorisation for questioning

(1) The court may authorise a constable to question a person about an offence after the person has been officially accused of committing the offence.

(2) The court may grant authorisation only if it is satisfied that allowing the person to be questioned about the offence is necessary in the interests of justice.

(3) In deciding whether to grant authorisation, the court must take into account—

(a) the seriousness of the offence,

(b) the extent to which the person could have been questioned earlier in relation to the information which the applicant believes may be elicited by the proposed questioning,

(c) where the person could have been questioned earlier in relation to that information, whether it could reasonably have been foreseen at that time that the information might be important to proving or disproving that the person has committed an offence.

(4) Where subsection (5) applies, the court must give the person an opportunity to make representations before deciding whether to grant authorisation.

(5) This subsection applies where—

(a) a warrant has been granted to arrest the person in respect of the offence, or

(b) the person has appeared before a court in relation to the offence.

(6) Where granting authorisation, the court—

(a) must specify the period for which questioning is authorised, and

(b) may specify such other conditions as the court considers necessary to ensure that allowing the proposed questioning is not unfair to the person.

(7) A decision of the court—

(a) to grant or refuse authorisation, or

(b) to specify, or not to specify, conditions under subsection (6)(b),

is final.

(8) In this section, 'the court' means—

(a) where an indictment has been served on the person in respect of the High Court, a single judge of that court,

(b) in any other case, the sheriff.

36 Authorisation: further provision

(1) An application for authorisation may be made—

(a) where section 35(5) applies, by the prosecutor, or

(b) in any other case, by a constable.

(2) In subsection (1)(a), 'the prosecutor' means—

(a) where an indictment has been served on the person in respect of the High Court, Crown Counsel, or

(b) in any other case, the procurator fiscal.

(3) Where an application for authorisation is made in writing (rather than orally) it must—

(a) be made in such form as may be prescribed by act of adjournal (or as nearly as may be in such form), and

(b) state whether another application has been made for authorisation to question the person about the offence or an offence arising from the same circumstances as the offence.

(4) Authorisation ceases to apply as soon as either—

(a) the period specified under section 35(6)(a) expires, or

(b) the person's trial in respect of the offence, or an offence arising from the same circumstances as the offence, begins.

(5) For the purpose of subsection (4)(b), a trial begins—

(a) in proceedings on indictment, when the jury is sworn,

(b) in summary proceedings, when the first witness for the prosecution is sworn.

(6) In this section—

'authorisation' means authorisation under section 35,

'the offence' means the offence referred to in section 35(1).

37 Arrest to facilitate questioning

(1) On granting authorisation under section 35, the court may also grant a warrant for the person's arrest if it seems to the court expedient to do so.

(2) The court must specify in a warrant granted under subsection (1) the maximum period for which the person may be detained under it.

(3) The person's detention under a warrant granted under subsection (1) must end as soon as—

(a) the period of the person's detention under the warrant becomes equal to the maximum period specified under subsection (2),

(b) the authorisation ceases to apply (see section 36(4)), or

(c) in the opinion of the constable responsible for the investigation into the offence referred to in section 35(1), there are no longer reasonable grounds for suspecting that the person has committed—

(i) that offence, or

(ii) an offence arising from the same circumstances as that offence.

(4) For the purpose of subsection (3)(a), the period of the person's detention under the warrant begins when the person—

(a) is arrested at a police station, or

(b) arrives at a police station, having been taken there in accordance with section 4.

(5) For the avoidance of doubt—

(a) if the person is on bail when a warrant under subsection (1) is granted, the order admitting the person to bail is not impliedly recalled by the granting of the warrant,

(b) if the person is on bail when arrested under a warrant granted under subsection (1)—

(i) despite being in custody by virtue of the warrant the person remains on bail for the purpose of section 24(5)(b) of the 1995 Act,

(ii) when the person's detention under the warrant ends, the bail order continues to apply as it did immediately before the person's arrest,

(c) if the person is subject to an undertaking given under section 25(2)(a), the person remains subject to the undertaking despite—

(i) the granting of a warrant under subsection (1),

(ii) the person's arrest and detention under it.

CHAPTER 5
RIGHTS OF SUSPECTS IN POLICE CUSTODY

Intimation and access to another person

38 Right to have intimation sent to other person

(1) A person in police custody has the right to have intimation sent to another person of—

(a) the fact that the person is in custody,

(b) the place where the person is in custody.

(2) Intimation under subsection (1) must be sent—

(a) where a constable believes that the person in custody is under 16 years of age, regardless of whether the person requests that it be sent,

(b) in any other case, if the person requests that it be sent.

(3) The person to whom intimation is to be sent under subsection (1) is—

(a) where a constable believes that the person in custody is under 16 years of age, a parent of the person,

(b) in any other case, an adult reasonably named by the person in custody.

(4) Intimation under subsection (1) must be sent—

(a) as soon as reasonably practicable, or

(b) if subsection (5) applies, with no more delay than is necessary.

(5) This subsection applies where an appropriate constable considers some delay to be necessary in the interests of—

(a) the investigation or prevention of crime,

(b) the apprehension of offenders, or

(c) safeguarding and promoting the wellbeing of the person in custody, where a constable believes that person to be under 18 years of age.

(6) In subsection (5), 'an appropriate constable' means a constable who—

(a) is of the rank of sergeant or above, and

(b) has not been involved in the investigation in connection with which the person is in custody.

(7) The sending of intimation may be delayed by virtue of subsection (5)(c) only for so long as is necessary to—

[(a)] ascertain whether a local authority will arrange for someone to visit the person in custody under section 41(2) [, or

(b) for a local authority to give advice by virtue of section 41(9).]

(8) In this section and section 39—

'adult' means person who is at least 18 years of age,

'parent' includes guardian and any person who has the care of the person in custody.

39 Right to have intimation sent: under 18s

(1) This section applies where a constable believes that a person in police custody is under 18 years of age.

(2) At the time of sending intimation to a person under section 38(1), that person must be asked to attend at the police station or other place where the person in custody is being held.

(3) Subsection (2) does not apply if—

(a) a constable believes that the person in custody is 16 or 17 years of age, and

(b) the person in custody requests that the person to whom intimation is to be sent under section 38(1) is not asked to attend at the place where the person in custody is being held.

(4) Subsections (5) and (6) apply where—

(a) it is not practicable or possible to contact, within a reasonable time, the person to whom intimation is to be sent by virtue of section 38(3),

(b) the person to whom intimation is sent by virtue of section 38(3), if asked to attend at the place where the person in custody is being held, claims to be unable or unwilling to attend within a reasonable time, or

(c) a local authority, acting under section 41(9)(a), has advised against sending intimation to the person to whom intimation is to be sent by virtue of section 38(3).

(5) Section 38(3) ceases to have effect.

(6) Attempts to send intimation to an appropriate person under section 38(1) must continue to be made until—

(a) an appropriate person is contacted and agrees to attend, within a reasonable time, at the police station or other place where the person in custody is being held, or

(b) if a constable believes that the person in custody is 16 or 17 years of age, the person requests that (for the time being) no further attempt to send intimation is made.

(7) In subsection (6), 'an appropriate person' means—

(a) if a constable believes that the person in custody is under 16 years of age, a person the constable considers appropriate having regard to the views of the person in custody,

(b) if a constable believes that the person in custody is 16 or 17 years of age, an adult who is named by the person in custody and to whom a constable is willing to send intimation without a delay by virtue of section 38(5)(a) or (b).

(8) The reference in subsection (4)(a) to its not being possible to contact a person within a reasonable time includes the case where, by virtue of section 38(5)(a) or (b), a constable delays sending intimation to the person.

40 Right of under 18s to have access to other person

(1) Access to a person in police custody who a constable believes is under 16 years of age must be permitted to—

(a) a parent of the person,

(b) where a parent is not available, a person sent intimation under section 38 in respect of the person in custody.

(2) Access to a person in police custody who a constable believes is 16 or 17 years of age must be permitted to a person sent intimation under section 38 in respect of the person in custody where the person in custody wishes to have access to the person sent intimation.

(3) Access to a person in custody under subsection (1) or (2) need not be permitted to more than one person at the same time.

(4) In exceptional circumstances, access under subsection (1) or (2) may be refused or restricted so far as the refusal or restriction is necessary—

(a) in the interests of—

(i) the investigation or prevention of crime, or

(ii) the apprehension of offenders, or

(b) for the wellbeing of the person in custody.

(5) A decision to refuse or restrict access to a person in custody under subsection (1) or (2) may be taken only by a constable who—

(a) is of the rank of sergeant or above, and

(b) has not been involved in the investigation in connection with which the person is in custody.

(6) In this section, 'parent' includes guardian and any person who has the care of the person in custody.

Vulnerable persons

42 Support for vulnerable persons

(1) Subsection (2) applies where—

(a) a person is in police custody,

(b) a constable believes that the person is 16 years of age or over, and

(c) owing to mental disorder, the person appears to the constable to be unable to—

(i) understand sufficiently what is happening, or

(ii) communicate effectively with the police.

(2) With a view to facilitating the provision of support of the sort mentioned in subsection (3) to the person as soon as reasonably practicable, the constable must ensure that

intimation of the matters mentioned in subsection (4) is sent to a person who the constable considers is suitable to provide the support.

(3) That is, support to—

(a) help the person in custody to understand what is happening, and

(b) facilitate effective communication between the person and the police.

(4) Those matters are—

(a) the place where the person is in custody, and

(b) that support of the sort mentioned in subsection (3) is, in the view of the constable, required by the person.

(5) In this section—

(a) 'mental disorder' has the meaning given by section 328 of the Mental Health (Care and Treatment) (Scotland) Act 2003,

(b) the references to the police are to any—

(i) constable, or

(ii) person appointed as a member of police staff under section 26(1) of the Police and Fire Reform (Scotland) Act 2012.

Intimation and access to a solicitor

43 Right to have intimation sent to solicitor

(1) A person who is in police custody has the right to have intimation sent to a solicitor of any or all of the following—

(a) the fact that the person is in custody,

(b) the place where the person is in custody,

(c) that the solicitor's professional assistance is required by the person,

(d) if the person has been officially accused of an offence—

(i) whether the person is to be released from custody, and

(ii) where the person is not to be released, the court before which the person is to be brought in accordance with section 21(2) and the date on which the person is to be brought before that court.

(2) Where the person requests that intimation be sent under subsection (1), the intimation must be sent as soon as reasonably practicable.

44 Right to consultation with solicitor

(1) A person who is in police custody has the right to have a private consultation with a solicitor at any time.

(2) In exceptional circumstances, the person's exercise of the right under subsection (1) may be delayed so far as that is necessary in the interests of—

(a) the investigation or the prevention of crime, or

(b) the apprehension of offenders.

(3) A decision to delay the person's exercise of the right under subsection (1) may be taken only by a constable who—

(a) is of the rank of sergeant or above, and

(b) has not been involved in the investigation in connection with which the person is in custody.

(4) In subsection (1), 'consultation' means consultation by such method as may be appropriate in the circumstances and includes (for example) consultation by telephone.

CHAPTER 6
POLICE POWERS AND DUTIES

Powers of police

45 Use of reasonable force

A constable may use reasonable force—

(a) to effect an arrest,

(b) when taking a person who is in police custody to any place.

46 Common law power of entry

Nothing in this Part affects any rule of law concerning the powers of a constable to enter any premises for any purpose.

47 Common law power of search etc.

(1) Nothing in this Part affects any rule of law by virtue of which a constable may exercise a power of the type described in subsection (2).

(2) The type of power is a power that a constable may exercise in relation to a person by reason of the person's having been arrested and charged with an offence by a constable.

(3) Powers of the type described in subsection (2) include the power to—

(a) search the person,

(b) seize any item in the person's possession,

(c) cause the person to participate in an identification procedure.

48 Power of search etc. on arrest

(1) A constable may exercise in relation to a person to whom subsection (2) applies any power of the type described in section 47(2) which the constable would be able to exercise by virtue of a rule of law if the person had been charged with the relevant offence by a constable.

(2) This subsection applies to a person who—

(a) is in police custody having been arrested without a warrant, and

(b) has not, since being arrested, been charged with an offence by a constable.

(3) In subsection (1), 'the relevant offence' means the offence in connection with which the person is in police custody.

49 Taking drunk persons to designated place

(1) Where—

(a) a person is liable to be arrested in respect of an offence by a constable without a warrant, and

(b) the constable is of the opinion that the person is drunk,

the constable may take the person to a designated place (and do so instead of arresting the person).

(2) Nothing done under subsection (1)—

(a) makes a person liable to be held unwillingly at a designated place, or

(b) prevents a constable from arresting the person in respect of the offence referred to in that subsection.

(3) In this section, 'designated place' is any place designated by the Scottish Ministers for the purpose of this section as a place suitable for the care of drunken persons.

Duties of police

50 Duty not to detain unnecessarily

A constable must take every precaution to ensure that a person is not unreasonably or unnecessarily held in police custody.

51 Duty to consider child's wellbeing

(1) Subsection (2) applies when a constable is deciding whether to—

(a) arrest a child,

(b) hold a child in police custody,

(c) interview a child about an offence which the constable has reasonable grounds to suspect the child of committing, or

(d) charge a child with committing an offence.

(2) In taking the decision, the constable must treat the need to safeguard and promote the wellbeing of the child as a primary consideration.

(3) For the purposes of this section, a child is a person who is under 18 years of age.

52 Duties in relation to children in custody

(1) A child who is in police custody at a police station is, so far as practicable, to be prevented from associating with any adult who is officially accused of committing an offence other than an adult to whom subsection (2) applies.

(2) This subsection applies to an adult if a constable believes that it may be detrimental to the wellbeing of the

child mentioned in subsection (1) to prevent the child and adult from associating with one another.

(3) For the purposes of this section—

'child' means person who is under 18 years of age,

'adult' means person who is 18 years of age or over.

53 Duty to inform Principal Reporter if child not being prosecuted

(1) Subsections (2) and (3) apply if—

(a) a person is being kept in a place of safety in accordance with section 22(2) when it is decided not to prosecute the person for any relevant offence, and

(b) a constable has reasonable grounds for suspecting that the person has committed a relevant offence.

(2) The Principal Reporter must be informed, as soon as reasonably practicable, that the person is being kept in a place of safety under subsection (3).

(3) The person must be kept in a place of safety under this subsection until the Principal Reporter makes a direction under section 65(2) of the Children's Hearings (Scotland) Act 2011.

(4) An offence is a 'relevant offence' for the purpose of subsection (1) if—

(a) it is the offence with which the person was officially accused, leading to the person being kept in the place of safety in accordance with section 22(2), or

(b) it is an offence arising from the same circumstances as the offence mentioned in paragraph (a).

(5) In this section, 'place of safety' has the meaning given in section 202(1) of the Children's Hearings (Scotland) Act 2011.

DOMESTIC ABUSE (SCOTLAND) ACT 2018
(2018, asp 5)

PART 1
OFFENCE AS TO DOMESTIC ABUSE

Engaging in course of abusive behaviour

1 Abusive behaviour towards partner or ex-partner

(1) A person commits an offence if—

(a) the person ('A') engages in a course of behaviour which is abusive of A's partner or ex-partner ('B'), and

(b) both of the further conditions are met.

(2) The further conditions are—

(a) that a reasonable person would consider the course of behaviour to be likely to cause B to suffer physical or psychological harm,

(b) that either—

(i) A intends by the course of behaviour to cause B to suffer physical or psychological harm, or

(ii) A is reckless as to whether the course of behaviour causes B to suffer physical or psychological harm.

(3) In the further conditions, the references to psychological harm include fear, alarm and distress.

2 What constitutes abusive behaviour

(1) Subsections (2) to (4) elaborate on section 1(1) as to A's behaviour.

(2) Behaviour which is abusive of B includes (in particular)—

(a) behaviour directed at B that is violent, threatening or intimidating,

(b) behaviour directed at B, at a child of B or at another person that either—

(i) has as its purpose (or among its purposes) one or more of the relevant effects set out in subsection (3), or

(ii) would be considered by a reasonable person to be likely to have one or more of the relevant effects set out in subsection (3).

(3) The relevant effects are of—

(a) making B dependent on, or subordinate to, A,

(b) isolating B from friends, relatives or other sources of support,

(c) controlling, regulating or monitoring B's day-to-day activities,

(d) depriving B of, or restricting B's, freedom of action,

(e) frightening, humiliating, degrading or punishing B.

(4) In subsection (2)—

(a) in paragraph (a), the reference to violent behaviour includes sexual violence as well as physical violence,

(b) in paragraph (b), the reference to a child is to a person who is under 18 years of age.

3 Extra-territorial jurisdiction

(1) An offence under section 1(1) can be constituted by a course of behaviour engaged in by A even if the course of behaviour occurs wholly or partly outside the United Kingdom.

(2) If the course of behaviour occurs wholly outside the United Kingdom—

(a) A may be prosecuted, tried and punished for the offence—

(i) in a sheriff court district in which A is apprehended or in custody, or

(ii) in a sheriff court district that is determined by the Lord Advocate,

as if the offence has been committed entirely in that district,

(b) the offence is, for all things incidental to or consequential on trial and punishment, deemed to have been committed entirely in that district.

(3) Subsections (1) and (2) apply only if A, when the course of behaviour occurs—

(a) is habitually resident in Scotland, or

(b) is a UK national.

(4) 'UK national' means someone who is, as referred to in the British Nationality Act 1981—

(a) a British citizen,

(b) a British overseas territories citizen, a British National (Overseas) or a British Overseas citizen, or

(c) a British subject or a British protected person.

Evidence, aggravation and defence

4 Evidence of impact on victim

(1) The commission of an offence under section 1(1) does not depend on the course of behaviour actually causing B to suffer harm of the sort mentioned in section 1(2).

(2) The operation of section 2(2)(b) does not depend on behaviour directed at someone actually having on B any of the relevant effects set out in section 2(3).

(3) Nothing done by or mentioned in subsection (1) or (2) prevents evidence from being led in proceedings for an offence under section 1(1) about (as the case may be)—

(a) harm actually suffered by B as a result of the course of behaviour, or

(b) effects actually had on B of behaviour directed at someone.

5 Aggravation in relation to a child

(1) This subsection applies where it is, in proceedings for an offence under section 1(1)—

(a) specified in the complaint or libelled in the indictment that the offence is aggravated by reason of involving a child, and

(b) proved that the offence is so aggravated.

(2) The offence is so aggravated if, at any time in the commission of the offence—

(a) A directs behaviour at a child, or

(b) A makes use of a child in directing behaviour at B.

(3) The offence is so aggravated if a child sees or hears, or is present during, an incident of behaviour that A directs at B as part of the course of behaviour.

(4) The offence is so aggravated if a reasonable person would consider the course of behaviour, or an incident of A's behaviour that forms part of the course of behaviour, to be likely to adversely affect a child usually residing with A or B (or both).

(5) For it to be proved that the offence is so aggravated, there does not need to be evidence that a child—

(a) has ever had any—

(i) awareness of A's behaviour, or

(ii) understanding of the nature of A's behaviour, or

(b) has ever been adversely affected by A's behaviour.

(6) Evidence from a single source is sufficient to prove that the offence is so aggravated.

(7) Where subsection (1) applies, the court must—

(a) state on conviction that the offence is so aggravated,

(b) record the conviction in a way that shows that the offence is so aggravated,

(c) take the aggravation into account in determining the appropriate sentence, and

(d) state—

(i) where the sentence imposed in respect of the offence is different from that which the court would have imposed if the offence were not so aggravated, the extent of and the reasons for that difference, or

(ii) otherwise, the reasons for there being no such difference.

(8) Each of subsections (2) to (4) operates separately along with subsection (5), but subsections (2) to (4) may be used in combination along with subsection (5).

(9) Nothing in subsections (2) to (5) prevents evidence from being led about—

(a) a child's observations of, or feelings as to, A's behaviour, or

(b) a child's situation so far as arising because of A's behaviour.

(10) In subsections (4) and (5), the references to adversely affecting a child include causing the child to suffer fear, alarm or distress.

(11) In this section, the references to a child are to a person who—

(a) is not A or B, and

(b) is under 18 years of age.

6 Defence on grounds of reasonableness

(1) In proceedings for an offence under section 1(1), it is a defence for A to show that the course of behaviour was reasonable in the particular circumstances.

(2) That is to be regarded as shown if—

(a) evidence adduced is enough to raise an issue as to whether the course of behaviour is as described in subsection (1), and

(b) the prosecution does not prove beyond reasonable doubt that the course of behaviour is not as described in subsection (1).

Presumption, alternative and penalty

7 Presumption as to the relationship

(1) In proceedings for an offence under section 1(1), the matter of B being A's partner or ex-partner is to be taken as established—

(a) according to the stating of the matter in the charge of the offence in the complaint or indictment, and

(b) unless the matter is challenged as provided for in subsection (2).

(2) The matter is challenged—

(a) in summary proceedings, by—

(i) preliminary objection before the plea is recorded, or

(ii) later objection as the court allows in special circumstances,

(b) in proceedings on indictment, by giving notice of a preliminary objection in accordance with section 71(2) or 72(6)(b)(i) of the Criminal Procedure (Scotland) Act 1995.

Meaning given to key expressions

10 Meaning of references to behaviour

(1) Subsections (2) to (4) explain what is meant by the references to behaviour in this Part.

(2) Behaviour is behaviour of any kind, including (for example)—

(a) saying or otherwise communicating something as well as doing something,

(b) intentionally failing—

(i) to do something,

(ii) to say or otherwise communicate something.

(3) Behaviour directed at a person is such behaviour however carried out, including (in particular)—

(a) by way of conduct towards property,

(b) through making use of a third party,

as well as behaviour in a personal or direct manner.

(4) A course of behaviour involves behaviour on at least two occasions.

11 Meaning of partner and ex-partner

(1) Subsections (2) and (3) describe who is a person's partner or ex-partner as referred to in this Part.

(2) Someone is a person's partner if they are—

(a) spouses or civil partners of each other,

(b) living together as if spouses of each other, or

(c) in an intimate personal relationship with each other.

(3) Whether someone is a person's ex-partner is to be determined accordingly.

HATE CRIME AND PUBLIC ORDER (SCOTLAND) ACT 2021
(2021, asp 14)

PART 1
AGGRAVATION OF OFFENCES BY PREJUDICE

1 Aggravation of offences by prejudice

(1) An offence is aggravated by prejudice if—

(a) where there is a specific victim of the offence—

(i) at the time of committing the offence, or immediately before or after doing so, the offender demonstrates malice and ill-will towards the victim, and

(ii) the malice and ill-will is based on the victim's membership or presumed membership of a group defined by reference to a characteristic mentioned in subsection (2), or

(b) whether or not there is a specific victim of the offence, the offence is motivated (wholly or partly) by malice and ill-will towards a group of persons based on the group being defined by reference to a characteristic mentioned in subsection (2).

(2) The characteristics are—

(a) age,

(b) disability,

(c) race, colour, nationality (including citizenship), or ethnic or national origins,

(d) religion or, in the case of a social or cultural group, perceived religious affiliation,

(e) sexual orientation,

(f) transgender identity,

(g) variations in sex characteristics.

(3) It is immaterial whether or not the offender's malice and ill-will is also based (to any extent) on any other factor.

(4) Evidence from a single source is sufficient to prove that an offence is aggravated by prejudice.

(5) In this section—

'membership', in relation to a group, includes association with members of that group,

'presumed' means presumed by the offender.

2 Consequences of aggravation by prejudice

(1) Subsection (2) applies where it is—

(a) libelled in an indictment, or specified in a complaint, that an offence is aggravated by prejudice, and

(b) proved that the offence is so aggravated.

(2) The court must—

(a) state on conviction—

(i) that the offence is aggravated by prejudice, and

(ii) the type of prejudice by which the offence is aggravated (by reference to one or more of the characteristics mentioned in section 1(2)),

(b) record the conviction in a way that shows—

(i) that the offence is aggravated by prejudice, and

(ii) the type of prejudice by which the offence is aggravated (by reference to one or more of the characteristics mentioned in section 1(2)),

(c) take the aggravation into account in determining the appropriate sentence, and

(d) state—

(i) where the sentence in respect of the offence is different from that which the court would have imposed if the offence were not so aggravated, the extent of and the reasons for that difference, or

(ii) otherwise, the reasons for there being no such difference.

3 Racially aggravated harassment

(1) A person commits an offence if the person—

(a) pursues a racially aggravated course of conduct which amounts to harassment of another person and—

(i) is intended to amount to harassment of that person, or

(ii) occurs in circumstances where it would appear to a reasonable person that it would amount to harassment of that person, or

(b) acts in a manner which is racially aggravated and which causes, or is intended to cause, another person alarm or distress.

(2) A course of conduct or an action is racially aggravated if—

(a) at the time of carrying out the course of conduct or action, or immediately before or after doing so—

(i) the offender demonstrates malice and ill-will towards the victim, and

(ii) the malice and ill-will is based on the victim's membership or presumed membership of a group defined by reference to race, colour, nationality (including citizenship), or ethnic or national origins, or

(b) the course of conduct or action is motivated (wholly or partly) by malice and ill-will towards a group of persons based on the group being defined by reference to race, colour, nationality (including citizenship), or ethnic or national origins.

(3) It is immaterial whether or not the offender's malice and ill-will is also based (to any extent) on any other factor.

(4) A course of conduct must involve conduct on at least two occasions.

(5) In this section—

'conduct' includes speech,

'harassment' of a person includes causing the person alarm or distress,

'membership', in relation to a group, includes association with members of that group,

'presumed' means presumed by the offender.

(6) A person who commits an offence under this section is liable—

(a) on summary conviction, to imprisonment for a term not exceeding 12 months or a fine not exceeding the statutory maximum (or both), or

(b) on conviction on indictment, to imprisonment for a term not exceeding 7 years or a fine (or both).

PART 3
OFFENCES RELATING TO STIRRING UP HATRED

Offences of stirring up hatred

4 Offences of stirring up hatred

(1) A person commits an offence if—

(a) the person—

(i) behaves in a manner that a reasonable person would consider to be threatening, abusive or insulting, or

(ii) communicates to another person material that a reasonable person would consider to be threatening, abusive or insulting, and

(b) either—

(i) in doing so, the person intends to stir up hatred against a group of persons based on the group being defined by reference to race, colour, nationality (including citizenship), or ethnic or national origins, or

(ii) a reasonable person would consider the behaviour or the communication of the material to be likely to result in hatred being stirred up against such a group.

(2) A person commits an offence if—

(a) the person—

(i) behaves in a manner that a reasonable person would consider to be threatening or abusive, or

(ii) communicates to another person material that a reasonable person would consider to be threatening or abusive, and

(b) in doing so, the person intends to stir up hatred against a group of persons based on the group being defined by reference to a characteristic mentioned in subsection (3).

(3) The characteristics are—

(a) age,

(b) disability,

(c) religion or, in the case of a social or cultural group, perceived religious affiliation,

(d) sexual orientation,

(e) transgender identity,

(f) variations in sex characteristics.

(4) It is a defence for a person charged with an offence under this section to show that the behaviour or the communication of the material was, in the particular circumstances, reasonable.

(5) For the purposes of subsection (4), in determining whether behaviour or communication was reasonable, particular regard must be had to the importance of the right to freedom of expression by virtue of Article 10 of the European Convention on Human Rights, including the general principle that the right applies to the expression of information or ideas that offend, shock or disturb.

(6) For the purposes of subsection (4), it is shown that the behaviour or the communication of the material was, in the particular circumstances, reasonable if—

(a) evidence adduced is enough to raise an issue as to whether that is the case, and

(b) the prosecution does not prove beyond reasonable doubt that it is not the case.

(7) For the purposes of subsections (1)(a)(i) and (2)(a)(i), a person's behaviour—

(a) includes behaviour of any kind and, in particular, things that the person says, or otherwise communicates, as well as things that the person does,

(b) may consist of—

(i) a single act, or

(ii) a course of conduct.

(8) For the purposes of subsections (1)(a)(ii) and (2)(a)(ii), the ways in which a person may communicate material to another person are by—

(a) displaying, publishing or distributing the material,

(b) giving, sending, showing or playing the material to another person,

(c) making the material available to another person in any other way.

(9) A person who commits an offence under this section is liable—

(a) on summary conviction, to imprisonment for a term not exceeding 12 months or a fine not exceeding the statutory maximum (or both), or

(b) on conviction on indictment, to imprisonment for a term not exceeding 7 years or a fine (or both).

9 Protection of freedom of expression

For the purposes of section 4(2), behaviour or material is not to be taken to be threatening or abusive solely on the basis that it involves or includes—

(a) discussion or criticism of matters relating to—

(i) age,

(ii) disability,

(iii) sexual orientation,

(iv) transgender identity,

(v) variations in sex characteristics,

(b) discussion or criticism relating to, or expressions of antipathy, dislike, ridicule or insult towards—

(i) religion, whether religions generally or a particular religion,

(ii) religious beliefs or practices, whether religious beliefs or practices generally or a particular religious belief or practice,

(iii) the position of not holding religious beliefs, whether religious beliefs generally or a particular religious belief,

(c) proselytising, or

(d) urging of persons to cease practising their religions.

PART 4
FURTHER PROVISION RELATING TO HATE CRIME

The characteristics

11 Meaning of the characteristics

(1) This section applies for the interpretation of sections 1, 4 and 9.

(2) A reference to age includes a reference to an age range.

(3) A disability is a physical or mental impairment of any kind.

(4) For the purposes of subsection (3) (but without prejudice to its generality), a medical condition which has, has had, or may have a substantial or long-term effect, or is of a progressive nature, is to be regarded as amounting to an impairment.

(5) A group defined by reference to religion is a group of persons defined by reference to—

(a) religious belief or lack of religious belief,

(b) membership of or adherence to a church or religious organisation,

(c) support for the culture or traditions of a church or religious organisation,

(d) participation in activities associated with such a culture or such traditions.

(6) A reference to sexual orientation is a reference to sexual orientation towards—

(a) persons of the same sex,

(b) persons of a different sex, or

(c) both persons of the same sex and persons of a different sex.

(7) A person is a member of a group defined by reference to transgender identity if the person is—

(a) a female-to-male transgender person,

(b) a male-to-female transgender person,

(c) a non-binary person,

(d) a person who cross-dresses,

and references to transgender identity are to be construed accordingly.

(8) A person is a member of a group defined by reference to variations in sex characteristics if the person is born with

physical and biological sex characteristics which, taken as a whole, are neither—

(a) those typically associated with males, nor

(b) those typically associated with females,

and references to variations in sex characteristics are to be construed accordingly.

PART II

INTERNATIONAL CONVENTIONS

EUROPEAN CONVENTION FOR THE PROTECTION OF HUMAN RIGHTS AND FUNDAMENTAL FREEDOMS (1950)

ARTICLE 6

Right to a fair trial

1. In the determination of his civil rights and obligations or of any criminal charge against him, everyone is entitled to a fair and public hearing within a reasonable time by an independent and impartial tribunal established by law. Judgment shall be pronounced publicly but the press and public may be excluded from all or part of the trial in the interests of morals, public order or national security in a democratic society, where the interests of juveniles or the protection of the private life of the parties so require, or to the extent strictly necessary in the opinion of the court in special circumstances where publicity would prejudice the interests of justice.

2. Everyone charged with a criminal offence shall be presumed innocent until proved guilty according to law.

3. Everyone charged with a criminal offence has the following minimum rights:

(a) to be informed promptly, in a language which he understands and in detail, of the nature and cause of the accusation against him;

(b) to have adequate time and facilities for the preparation of his defence;

(c) to defend himself in person or through legal assistance of his own choosing or, if he has not sufficient means to pay for legal assistance, to be given it free when the interests of justice so require;

(d) to examine or have examined witnesses against him and to obtain the attendance and examination of witnesses on his behalf under the same conditions as witnesses against him;

(e) to have the free assistance of an interpreter if he cannot understand or speak the language used in court.

ARTICLE 10

Freedom of expression

1. Everyone has the right to freedom of expression. This right shall include freedom to hold opinions and to receive and impart information and ideas without interference by public authority and regardless of frontiers. This Article shall not prevent States from requiring the licensing of broadcasting, television or cinema enterprises.

2. The exercise of these freedoms, since it carries with it duties and responsibilities, may be subject to such formalities, conditions, restrictions or penalties as are prescribed by law and are necessary in a democratic society, in the interests of national security, territorial integrity or public safety, for the prevention of disorder or crime, for the protection of health or morals, for the protection of the reputation or rights of others, for preventing the disclosure of information received in confidence, or for maintaining the authority and impartiality of the judiciary.

ARTICLE 11

Freedom of assembly and association

1. Everyone has the right to freedom of peaceful assembly and to freedom of association with others, including the right to form and to join trade unions for the protection of his interests.

2. No restrictions shall be placed on the exercise of these rights other than such as are prescribed by law and are

necessary in a democratic society in the interests of national security or public safety, for the prevention of disorder or crime, for the protection of health or morals or for the protection of the rights and freedoms of others. This Article shall not prevent the imposition of lawful restrictions on the exercise of these rights by members of the armed forces, of the police or of the administration of the State.

INDEX OF MATERIALS